# FRANCIS ATTERBURY (1662-1732), BISHOP OF ROCHESTER, AND HIS FRENCH CORRESPONDENTS

**FRANCIS ATTERBURY, BISHOP OF ROCHESTER**
Portrait by Sir Godfrey Kneller

Courtesy of The National Portrait Gallery, London, England

# FRANCIS ATTERBURY (1662-1732), BISHOP OF ROCHESTER, AND HIS FRENCH CORRESPONDENTS

Rex A. Barrell

Studies in British History
Volume 19

The Edwin Mellen Press
Lewiston/Queenston/Lampeter

BX
5199
.A87
A4
1990

Library of Congress Cataloging-in-Publication Data

Atterbury, Francis, 1662-1732.
  Francis Atterbury (1662-1732), Bishop of Rochester, and his French correspondents / [edited by] Rex A. Barrell.
    p. cm. -- (Studies in British history ; v. 19)
  Correspondence in Latin with English translations and notes.
  Includes bibliographical references.
  ISBN 0-88946-451-0
  1. Atterbury, Francis, 1662-1732--Correspondence. 2. Church of England--France--Bishops--Correspondence. 3. Anglican Communion--Bishops--Correspondence. 4. Jacobites--Correspondence. 5. Great Britain--Exiles--Correspondence. 6. France--Exiles--Correspondence. 7. Great Britain--Politics and government--1714-1760. 8. French literature--16th century--History and criticism. 9. French literature--17th century--History and criticism. I. Barrell, Rex A. II. Title. III. Series.
BX5199.A87A4 1990
283'.092--dc20                                              89-48245
                                                                CIP

---

This is volume 19 in the continuing series
Studies in British History
Volume 19   ISBN 0-88946-451-0
SBH Series  ISBN 0-88946-450-2

---

A CIP catalog record for this book
is available from the British Library.

Copyright ©1990 The Edwin Mellen Press
All rights reserved. For information contact

The Edwin Mellen Press          The Edwin Mellen Press
       Box 450                          Box 67
  Lewiston, New York              Queenston, Ontario
     USA 14092                    CANADA, L0S 1L0

The Edwin Mellen Press, Ltd.
Lampeter, Dyfed, Wales
UNITED KINGDOM SA48 7DY

Printed in the United States of America

FOR

ROSALIND

AND

LLOYD

TABLE OF CONTENTS

| PREFACE | i |
|---|---|
| INTRODUCTION | vii |
| BIOGRAPHICAL SKETCH | 1 |
| CORRESPONDENCE - THIERIOT | 15 |
| VOLTAIRE | 43 |
| CORRESPONDENCE - CAUMONT | 49 |
| CORRESPONDENCE - ROLLIN | 59 |
| BIBLIOGRAPHY | 65 |
| INDEX | 71 |

# PREFACE

In the establishment of the text, I have observed the following principles:

1. <u>Orthography</u>

The original spelling has been retained, but I replace letters no longer used (lengthened 's' and double 's') by their modern equivalents, and I adopt the modern distinction between 'i' and 'j'; 'u' and 'v'.

2. <u>Accentuation</u>

In general no accents are added or changed. However, I supply an accent where interpretation can be confusing (e.g. 'ou', or 'où'), as opposed to the case where an unaccented vowel (such as 'a' used as a preposition) leaves the meaning perfectly clear (e.g. 'a Paris'). Stress accents on words in Latin quotations have been removed (e.g. 'consulto' for 'consultò').

3. <u>Punctuation</u>

Commas are inserted or removed only to facilitate understanding. Apostrophes are regularised.

4. <u>Capitalization</u>

I preserve the capitals that were used so indiscriminately in both English and French letters of the period, but I add capitals to proper names, names of nationality and to words beginning a sentence where these are not present. I make an exception with Latin quotations and letters where I give capitals only to nationalities, titles, nouns purposely stressed, and words beginning sentences.

5. <u>Paragraphing</u>

While largely maintaining the author's own system of indentation, I increase the number of paragraphs on occasion in order to lighten a dense text.

6. Grammar

Grammatical peculiarities as well as obvious errors are mentioned in the textual notes.

7. Dating

Letters have been dated according to the Gregorian Calendar (N.S.) which England adopted only in 1752. Up to 1700, the difference between the Julian (O.S.) and Gregorian dates was ten days; after this date it was eleven. Until 1752, the first day of the year was regularly dated March 25 in England. For this reason it must be noted that Atterbury was born in England in 1662 (O.S.), and died in France in 1732 (N.S.)

As for the critical apparatus, I use three main headings: sources (manuscript and/or printed), textual notes and commentary.

The following abbreviations are used:

Bailey: D. R. Shackleton Bailey (ed.), Cicero's Letters to Atticus, Cambridge, University Press, 1965-70, 7 vols.

Beeching: H. C. Beeching, Francis Atterbury, London, Pitman & Sons, 1909.

Bennett: Gareth V. Bennett, The Tory Crisis in Church and State 1688-1730. The Career of Francis Atterbury, Bishop of Rochester, Oxford, Clarendon Press, 1975.

Besterman: 1. Theodore Besterman (ed.), Correspondence of Voltaire, Oxford, Voltaire Foundation, 1968-77 (Vols. 85-135 of the Oeuvres complètes).

2. Theodore Besterman (éd.), Oeuvres complètes de Voltaire, Oxford, Voltaire Foundation, 1968---

Desfontaines: L'Esprit de l'Abbé Des Fontaines ou Reflexions sur differens genres de science et de litterature, éd. l'Abbé de la Porte, Paris, 1757.

CH MSS: The Cholmondeley (Houghton) papers, deposited in the Cambridge University Library.

Coxe: William Coxe, Memoirs of the Life and Administration of Sir Robert Walpole, Earl of Orford, London, T. Cadell & W. Davies, 1798, 3 vols.

Dobrée: Bonamy Dobrée, The Letters of Lord Chesterfield, London, Eyre & Spottiswoode, 1932, 6 vols.

Fr. Roffen: Franciscus Roffensis (Francis of Rochester).

Hearne: The Remains of Thomas Hearne (ed. J. Bliss), London, Centaur Press Ltd., 1966.

HMC: The Historical Manuscripts Commission

Macaulay: Thomas Babington Macaulay, Encyclopaedia Britannica 1853 (Article on Francis Atterbury). (The same article in substance appeared in Macaulay's Biographies, Edinburgh, A & C Black, 1867).

Nichols: John Nichols (ed.) The Miscellaneous Works of Bishop Atterbury, London, 1789-98, 5 vols.

(Pope) Corr.: The Correspondence of Alexander Pope (ed. George Sherburn), 1956, 5 vols.

R.A. Stuart: The Royal Archives, Windsor Castle (where are housed the Stuart papers 5-163).

SVEC: Studies on Voltaire and the Eighteenth Century, ed. T. Besterman (1955-76), H. Mason (1977---), Geneva and later Banbury, 1955---.

Williams: R. Folkestone Williams (ed.), Memoirs and Correspondence of Francis Atterbury, D.D., Bishop of Rochester, London, W. H. Allen & Co., 1869, 2 vols.

Finally, it gives me great pleasure to make the following acknowledgements:

To: Mr. James P. Derriman, my research assistant in London, England, who kindly copied letters and other material and who performed many services in a most efficient and professional manner.

To: Professor Padraig O'Cleirigh of the Department of Languages and Literatures (Classics Section) at Guelph, for his assistance in locating and translating classical references and in translating the two Latin letters to Caumont and to Rollin.

To: Mme Françoise de Forbin, archivist at the Municipal Library of Avignon, for graciously providing a photocopy of Atterbury's letter to the Marquis de Caumont, and for giving me permission to publish it.

To: The Archivist Staff, Historical Division, at the Ministry of Foreign Affairs, Quai d'Orsay, Paris, for instituting an historical search.

v

To: M. Jean Favier, the Director-General of the <u>Archives de France</u>, for attempting to unearth Atterbury documents transferred to the <u>Archives</u> from Scots College in Paris.

To: The editors of <u>Notes and Queries</u> for kindly publishing my query concerning the whereabouts of missing Atterbury correspondence.

To: Mlle Yvonne Rateau of Paris, France, for her constant loyalty and assistance.

To: Mlle Colette Dethan of the <u>Service Visites et Information</u> of the <u>Bibliothèque Nationale</u> in Paris for photocopying correspondence and performing other services.

To: Mr. Ian Hill, Historical Search Room of the Scottish Record Office in Edinburgh, for help in endeavouring to locate Atterbury's papers in the archives of the Scots College in Paris.

To the following for many useful suggestions, services and advice:

Professor Leonard Adams of the Department of Languages and Literatures at Guelph.

Professor Pierre Marie Conlon of the Department of French at McMaster University in Hamilton.

Professor E. J. Cowan of the Department of History at Guelph.

The Rev. Dr. Geoffrey Rowell, Chaplain of Keble College, Oxford.

Professor André-Michel Rousseau of Aix en Provence.

The Rev. Michael Smith, St. David's Vicarage, Exeter.

To: The Staff of the University of Guelph Library, who performed invaluable service in obtaining inter-library loans and locating bibliographical resources.

To: The National Portrait Gallery, London, England, for kindly allowing me to reproduce a portrait of Atterbury.

To: The Social Sciences and Humanities Research Council of Canada for generously awarding me a research grant to carry out this study.

To: Mrs. Janice Walker for her most prompt and efficient services in word-processing the MS.

# INTRODUCTION

Modern research on Francis Atterbury, Bishop of Rochester (1662-1732) has concentrated on his controversial life as a cleric, orator, scholar and Jacobite sympathizer who was exiled for treason in 1723 and spent the remainder of his life in France. His main activities during this exile were directed towards political matters, but he did frequent a wide circle of acquaintances many of whom were distinguished authors and scholars such as Charles Rollin the historian and rector of the University of Paris, the Abbé Desfontaines, distinguished Anglophile and classicist, the Abbé Vertot historian of political movements and institutions, the Abbé Granet, review collaborator and literary critic, editor of French classical authors and translator of Newton, le Père Montfaucon, Benedictine scholar, hellenist and prolific writer, the Marquis de Caumont, archeologist, antiquarian and collaborator of the Journal de Trévoux, le Père (Le) Courayer, renegade cleric whose sympathy with and work on Anglicanism earned him an exile in England, and Thieriot, friend of Voltaire and literary correspondent. Of these literary figures Thieriot, Rollin, Le Courayer, the Abbé Desfontaines, the Abbé Granet and the Marquis de Caumont were his chief correspondents, and since only the Thieriot exchange has been published (though insufficiently annotated), it seemed a worthwhile idea to attempt to track down letters to other writers. Unfortunately many of Atterbury's papers and documents, sealed by the French Ministry of Justice, were destroyed after his death for political reasons, some letters were returned to their owners and the rest transferred to Scots College in Paris. On the demise of this institution, most were likely destroyed or scattered, and their present whereabouts is a matter of conjecture. Extensive inquiries have failed to turn up more than a handful; these and the Thieriot letters form the basis of the present study.

During Atterbury's lifetime, only sketchy reports of his career appeared in print, due to the refusal of the British Government, the Jacobites, and those intimately involved in his political misfortunes to release information. An incomplete study by Thomas Stackhouse entitled Memoirs of the life and conduct of Dr. Francis Atterbury dealing with his career up to and including his trial, was published in 1723 and re-edited in 1727. In the second edition of Vol. I of the Biographica Britannica, 1778, appeared a reasonably objective assessment of Atterbury with notes considerably more extensive than the actual text by Andrew Kippis. It was only in 1783 however that John Nichols began to edit and publish papers in private possession, a project which led to the five volumes of the Miscellaneous Works of Bishop Atterbury published from 1789 to 1798. In 1847, J. H. Glover published the earlier Atterbury letters in the Stuart papers printed from the originals in Windsor. Macaulay's well-known article in the Encyclopaedia Britannica of 1853 was based on all these sources and gives a clear, if biased, summary of Atterbury's life and career. A collection entitled Memoirs and Correspondence of Francis Atterbury, Bishop of Rochester was produced in two volumes, edited by R. Folkestone Williams in 1869, but this added very little to previous publications, and in the words of Bennett, the narrative 'joined wild surmise to gross error'. (viii) A more accurate and objective biography making use of the Historical Manuscripts Commission Publications available at that date was produced in 1909 by Canon H. C. Beeching. The present standard biography using materials recently discovered and unavailable to Beeching, appeared in 1975 (Oxford, Clarendon Press). It is entitled The Tory Crisis in Church and State: The Career of Francis Atterbury, Bishop of Rochester, and is the work of Gareth V. Bennett, a former scholar and teacher at New College, Oxford.

BIOGRAPHICAL SKETCH

Born on March 6, 1662 at Middleton or Milton-Keynes near Newport-Pagnell in Buckinghamshire, England, a parish where his father, Lewis Atterbury, was an undistinguished parson, Francis was educated at Westminster school under the famed Dr. Busby and then at Christ Church College, Oxford in 1680. An extremely diligent student, he soon distinguished himself by his elegant taste and his rapid mastery of classical literature; at the early age of 20 he produced a Latin version of Dryden's Absalom and Achitophel entitled <u>Absalom & Achitophel Poema Latino Carmine donatum</u> which was published in 1682. This was followed by an epigram on a lady's fan written between the sticks and a translation of two Odes of Horace (Ode 9, Bk. 3 and Ode 3, Bk. 4). The degree of Bachelor of Arts was awarded him in June 1684 and that of Master of Arts in April of 1687, the year in which he produced his first piece of controversial writing, <u>An Answer to some Considerations of the Spirit of Martin Luther, and the Original of the Reformation</u>, a response to the tract of Obadiah Walker. Written with wit and vivacity, it vindicated all of Luther's doctrines, inducing Bishop Burnet to rank Atterbury amongst the eminent Divines who had defended the Protestant religion against the attacks of Popery. During his University years, Atterbury is generally thought to have taken a significant role in the controversy between the great scholar Richard Bentley and the Honourable Charles Boyle, grandson of the first Earl of Orrery and nephew of Robert Boyle the experimental philosopher, concerning the authenticity of Phalaris's Epistles, an edition of which Boyle had prepared. The response to Bentley's dissertation in which he proved that the Epistles were spurious and a new edition of them written under the name of Boyle worthless, was so impregnated with a fine sense of raillery and polished wit that it is generally acknowledged to have been chiefly the work of Atterbury, and, according to Macaulay (p. 53), his masterpiece.

Tiring of the controversies of College life despite his success as a tutor, Atterbury began in 1693 to seek clerical preferment and soon distinguished himself in such a manner that he was appointed one of the Chaplains in Ordinary to King William and Queen Mary, being elected at the same time preacher at Bridewell and Lecturer of St. Bride's. In 1694 his two renowned sermons, The Power of Charity to cover Sin and The Scorner incapable of True Wisdom, the latter preached before the Queen at Whitehall, earned him critical acclaim from some but intense hostility from others. In 1695 he married Miss Catherine Osborne, the daughter of a country parson near Oxford, and in his new house in Chelsea his three children were born, Mary, Elizabeth and Francis. Party spirit in these years ran high, Atterbury belonging to the Christ Church stronghold of Toryism and Bentley to the Whigs, but this conflict took second place to the bitter hostility between religious factions; the High Church and Low Church split the nation with most of the clergy including Atterbury on the High Church side, while the majority of the King's bishops, including Dr. William Wake, later Archbishop of Canterbury, tended towards latitudinarianism. The controversy between Atterbury and Wake and others concerning the rights, powers and privileges of Convocations lasted four years and won him the gratitude of the Lower House of Convocation as well as the degree of Doctor of Divinity from the University of Oxford. Archdeacon of Totness in 1700 on the recommendation of Sir Jonathan Trelawny, then Bishop of Exeter, he became, on the accession of Queen Anne in 1702, one of her Chaplains in Ordinary and in 1704 was promoted to the Deanery of Carlisle. Further appointments followed: a Canon Residentiary of the Church in Exeter in 1707 and preacher of the Rolls-Chapel in 1707, but these posts did not prevent him from avidly pursuing his classical studies (in 1700 he was engaged with other Divines in a revised edition of the Greek testament).

    Closely involved in the famous trial of Dr. Henry Sacheverell whose notorious speech was a mish-mash of the sermons of others including Dr. Smalridge, Dr. Freind and himself, he was rewarded by being chosen Prolocutor of the Lower House of Convocation in which capacity he managed the affairs of the House. In June of 1711, Atterbury was chiefly responsible for drawing up A Representation of the present State of Religion, a virulent criticism of all the

administrations from the time of the Revolution and a
powerful attack on the atheism and irreligion of the times.
The same year he was made Dean of Christ Church and in
1713, on the recommendation of the Earl of Oxford, he
reached the pinnacle of his career as Bishop of Rochester
and Dean of Westminster. Held in high esteem by the
Queen and the Ministry, he schemed to achieve his ultimate
goal of Primate of England, but with the death of Queen
Anne in 1714, his fortunes took a serious down-turn.
George I sensed his hostility to the House of Hanover and
took a personal dislike to him. During the rebellion of 1715
in Scotland, Atterbury showed his growing disaffection to
the Government by refusing to sign the Bishops' <u>Declaration</u>,
testifying their abhorrence of the Rebellion and exhorting
the Clergy and populace to support the new King.
Thereafter Atterbury appears to have lost his judgement
completely, passing a great deal of his time in factious
debate and writing. Although his brilliant oratory in the
House of Lords frequently held the members spellbound, he
could not succeed in mastering his own vindictive nature,
and it was not long before he decided to throw in his lot
with the Pretender with whose family he had long been in
indirect communication. In 1721 the Jacobite spirit appeared
to revive after the débâcle of 1715. Discontent in England,
due to the failure of the South Sea project, the panic in
the money market which caused the downfall of many great
commercial houses and the general distress of the nation,
led Atterbury to believe that an insurrection might this time
be successful. Indeed this was in the planning stages and
might have had some measure of success had not the Regent
of France, the Duc d'Orléans, who was on terms of
friendship with the House of Hanover, got wind of it and
informed the Government. In 1772 Sir Robert Walpole took
a very active role in denouncing Atterbury before the
House, clearly proving that he was directly involved in a
plot to overthrow the present regime. Atterbury was
apprehended and committed to the Tower and, despite a
most eloquent speech in his own defence, the Bill 'inflicting
certain pains and penalties on Francis Lord Bishop of
Rochester' was passed by 83 to 43 and confirmed by the
King himself. On June 18, 1723, Atterbury went into
perpetual banishment in Europe, a victim, as Bolingbroke

had been before him, of his own machinations.

On June 21 the Aldborough berthed at Calais, and accompanied by his daughter Mary and her husband William Morrice (Morice), Atterbury stepped ashore unheralded and unwelcomed. By an ironic twist of fate, Bolingbroke was, at that very moment, lodged in a hotel in the same town awaiting the ship that would return him to England at the end of his own period of exile. 'Then, I am exchanged!' Atterbury was reported as exclaiming with grim resentment. Hearing of Atterbury's arrival, Bolingbroke pretended to be sick so as to avoid meeting a man whom he no longer trusted. Having claimed to renounce Jacobitism, he did not want to be embroiled in Atterbury's affairs (Letter to Townshend, circa Feb. 1, 1724, Coxe, vol. II, p. 327). The Bishop had planned to settle in Brussels where he hoped to make contact with a few English Jacobites and to offer his services to the Pretender, and the little party arrived in the Belgian capital on June 27. The stay of three months in a gloomy lodging hastily rented, was one of the worst periods of his life. Crippled by the gout which the damp climate of Brussels did nothing to alleviate, afflicted with deep depression as the full realization of his miserable position came over him, seemingly abandoned by his English friends and unable to make new acquaintances easily as a result of his lack of fluency in French, he felt that the world had passed him by. As it turned out, he was still very much at the centre of English concern. Walpole sent John Mackay, an experienced spy, to dog his every step, and every week reports on Atterbury's visitors, activities and opinions were transmitted to London. The Pretender, who was at this period in Rome, sent affectionate letters to the Bishop urging him to join him in Italy and recover his health in the sun. His own affairs were at an impasse: two rival factions were at loggerheads. On the one hand the Earl of Mar appeared to be in control in Paris and on the other James Murray and John Hay were complaining of gross mismanagement of James's affairs. Hay was sent from Rome to Paris to ask Atterbury's help in formulating a new policy in France; Hay would become Secretary of State with the title of Earl of Inverness and Atterbury would be the new Minister in Paris. Atterbury agreed and appeared to take a new lease of life. Mar, supported by General Dillon and Lansdowne who fancied himself as a literary figure, had given Atterbury trouble before, and he was anxious to supplant him.

Travelling via Cambrai, where his arrival surprised members of an important diplomatic congress which had gathered in the town, Atterbury reached Paris on May 20 and settled into temporary lodgings, hiring furniture and a sedan chair to convey him about. Horatio Walpole, the British Ambassador, pressed by his brother Sir Robert, had attempted to have him expelled from France, providing a spy to watch his every movement, but the French Government merely decided to ignore his presence. A painful interview with Mar during which the latter consented to handing over his official papers, led to the Earl's dismissal from James' service as a double agent. Atterbury's loyalty to the Pretender was as ill-starred as that of Bolingbroke's a few years previously. The planned uprising in England and Scotland fell through as a result of treachery, double-dealing and mismanagement, Atterbury's final hope of a grand alliance of Spain, Austria and Russia which could be persuaded into a war against England was never realized, and the quarrel between the Pretender and his wife Clementina over the Protestant tutor of their son threatened to ruin James completely in the eyes of his English Protestant subjects, while the constant surveillance by spies most of whom were double agents caused utter confusion for Atterbury's well-laid schemes and blackened his reputation further in both countries. The most well-known of these spies was John Sample, a young Irishman who, under the guise of a confidant, submitted a thrice-weekly report on Atterbury's visitors and activities from mid 1724 to the end of 1731. Even James himself proved treacherous to his own Minister, thus shattering the Bishop's faith in his personal integrity. When, at the end of May 1727, Britain, France and Austria signed the preliminaries for a new peace treaty in Paris, Atterbury realized that it was all over and, with unusual calm and resignation, he sent in his letter of resignation. Once again, as in Bolingbroke's case, it must be noted that Atterbury had no respect for Roman Catholicism as a religion. His real loyalty was not to the

Stuart regime but to an outdated vision of a Church and State alliance which his Oxford education had given him. Bennett puts it succinctly (p. 225):

> "It was Atterbury's tragedy that, in spite of his great religious and pastoral gifts, he was convinced that the well-being of the Church of England was still primarily bound up with the political regime and that her cause was best furthered by political agitation. When all had failed in England, he turned to the Stuarts as the one means by which the ecclesiastical past might be restored."

Despite Atterbury's busy life as a Jacobite politician and diplomat, he found time to cultivate French men of letters and pursue his academic interests. Thomas Hearne, an historical antiquary and good friend of the Bishop, notes that right from his arrival in Paris he frequented the public libraries and other curiosities of the city, and that he was visited by most of the members of the Royal Academy of Sciences, by le Père Montfaucon, Abbé Vertot and 'other persons of Distinction and Learning, who seem to pay him more than ordinary respect'. (Hearne, Aug. 9, 1724, p. 273, quoted by Beeching, p. 323, who, however, gives the date as August, 1723). The writer of a letter to the Daily Post of July 17, 1737 which was sent by a Frenchman but published in English, is incontrovertible evidence of Atterbury's popularity with the clergy who tried to outdo the men of letters in their attentions:

> "When he was in France [states the writer], what respect, what caresses did he not receive from the Dignified Clergy! what pains, what industry, what arguments did they not employ to bring him over to their communion! This was a point which they pursued several years together, even to his last moments, with an assiduity altogether as indefatigable as it was fruitless".

(Quoted by Beeching, pp. 323-4).

Again, according to Beeching who is not altogether convinced of the truth of the report (p. 324), the doctors of the Sorbonne sent a select deputation to Atterbury to invite him to a conference on the subject of the differences between the Protestant and Catholic churches, hoping to convince him of the sinfulness of dissension from their apostolic faith. Atterbury outlined the problem of the differences between various texts of the Vulgate sanctioned by Popes all equally infallible. In the <u>Nouveau Dictionnaire Historique</u> (1772), we read the following eulogy of Atterbury's learning, taste and urbanity:

> "Cet eveque, retiré en France, fut le conseil et l'ami des gens de lettres; il s'en fit recherché par son erudition et par son goût, et aimé par sa politesse et les agrémens de son commerce."

> (Quoted by Beeching, p. 323)

His friend and correspondent Abbé Desfontaines, eulogizes Atterbury's elegant and pure Latin, his profound knowledge of the classical authors of the reign of Augustus as well as of the literature of French classicism, and his appreciation of, if not his fluency in the French language:

> "---il parloit Latin avec une élégance & une pureté dont j'ose dire que peu de gens ont approché. Personne n'a jamais si bien possédé les belles Lettres, ni mieux senti la finesse et la délicatesse des Auteurs du Regne d'<u>Auguste</u>, qu'il lisoit continuellement. Ç'a été sans contredit un des plus beaux esprits d'Angleterre. Il avoit lû nos meilleurs Ecrivains & sur-tout les Ouvrages du grand <u>Bossuet</u>, dont il étoit l'admirateur, ainsi que de <u>Boileau</u> & de <u>Rousseau</u>. Quoiqu'il ne parlât point notre Langue, il en connaissoit le génie & les beautés. Nulle faute ne lui échappoit, & j'ai souvent été étonné de sa sagacité en ce point. Lorsque M. <u>de la Motte</u> se déclara

contre la rime de notre versification, il
s'entretenoit avec plaisir sur cette matiére;
mais quoiqu'il ne goutât pas plus la rime
que cet Académicien, il disoit que M. de la
Motte n'avoit pas assez de capacité pour
trouver dans notre Langue une harmonie
équivalente. . . . M. Atterbury étoit un
Sçavant aimable, poli & d'un commerce
agréable; il n'avoit rien de cette rudesse
sauvage qui caractérise les Sçavans"
(Desfontaines, pp. 126-7).

As is evident in Atterbury's letters collected by
John Nichols, his interest in all aspects of literature
continued unabated through these years of exile. Writing to
the Duke of Wharton on Aug. 26, 1725 (Williams, vol. II,
p. 188), the young English aristocrat who had come to his
defence in London and who had been conscripted to the
Jacobite cause in Vienna, Atterbury urges him to read the
letters of Cardinal d'Ossat as a model of acting and writing
in all matters of negotiation. He could read them in a late
French edition by Amelot de La Houssaye or in a Dutch
edition and would find them 'equal entertainment and
instruction-a mixture of wisdom and honesty, both in the
height'. It is interesting to note that some twenty years
later the fourth Earl of Chesterfield also recommended these
letters for their simplicity and clarity to his budding
diplomat son (Lettre à son fils, 20 juillet 1747, Dobrée, vol.
III, p. 968). Atterbury also noted the practice of translating
foreign epic poems into French prose. In the case of
Milton whose two great works (Paradise Lost and Paradise
Regained) had been translated into French prose by Dupré
de Saint-Maur, and retranslated into English, Atterbury
seemed convinced that the cultural shock of the original
would soon pass and the epics rise higher in French esteem
at Paris (Letter to Mr. Morrice, May 31, 1729, Nichols, vol.
IV, Letter LXXVI, pp. 228-9). On the occasion of Chevalier
Ramsay's book Travels of Cyrus with a Discourse on
Mythology (2 vols. 1727), there is a reference to Montaigne
in a letter to Mrs. Morrice of March 16, 1728. Atterbury
states that 'un peu de chaque chose, et rien du tout à la
Françoise' would be properly placed in the first page of

Cyrus (Nichols, vol. IV, Letter XLIV, p. 114). Atterbury's relations with his friend Thieriot and through him with Voltaire, will be discussed when we deal with the extant correspondence.

During his exile, Atterbury continued his daily pastoral activities with the Anglicans abroad as well as attempting to organize a system of Jacobite chaplaincies to ensure that there was some pastor in each of the chief European capitals. Even these efforts were attended with problems and disappointments, and he often had to adjudicate in quarrels of the Nonjuring clergy many of whom made unwanted innovations in liturgical matters. In a letter of Sample to Horatio Walpole of June 7, 1726, Atterbury appeared to suffer from the harassment of over-zealous priests who attempted to convert him to Roman Catholicism, a religion which never ceased to be anathema to him (Ch MSS 1338). To avoid embarrassment he refused to enter Paris churches and to receive visitors other than those in whose company he could confine his conversation to literature and the arts. The only French priest with whom Atterbury became intimate was Pierre François Le Courayer, the Canon-Regular and librarian of Sainte-Geneviève who was a convinced protagonist of the Church of England, having in 1721 written a learned dissertation on the validity of Anglican Orders (<u>Dissertation sur la Validité des Ordinations des Anglais</u>, Bruxelles (Nancy), 1723) which was translated by D. Williams in 1725 and caused a furore in Paris. So bitter was the hostility of the Jesuits who saw in the work a justification of Jansenist doctrine that Le Courayer engaged Atterbury to work on the outlines of a <u>Défense</u> which finally appeared in 1726 at Brussels (<u>Défense de la Dissertation sur la Validité des Ordinations des Anglais contre les différentes réponses qui y ont été faites</u>), also translated by Williams in 1728. Except for a laudatory article by Pierre Des Molets in the <u>Nouvelles littéraires</u> of Dec. 1, 1723, both works were severely criticized in France. Chief among the detractors were two celebrated clerics, the Jesuit le Père Hardouin, and the Dominican le Révérend-Père Michel Le Quien whose rebuttals of Le Courayer's heterodoxical belief in a possible union between the Gallican and Anglican Churches, while making some valid points from a theological point of view, were historically unconvincing and in parts invalid. A commission of twenty bishops officially condemned Le Courayer's <u>Dissertation</u> making scathing comments on the whole Anglican doctrine. Atterbury was outraged and considered writing a lengthy justification of his friend's views, even more convinced that the Church of Rome was opposed to the two great virtues he cherished: truth and charity. His better judgement prevailed however, since any criticism from the pen of an exiled Bishop in a foreign country would sit ill with the authorities. It is interesting to picture the two friends planning and plotting their strategies, either in Atterbury's Paris residence or in Senlis where Le Courayer had been given permission to visit friends, or at the Priory of Hennemont in the Commune of St. Germain en Laye where he had been authorized to take a retreat.

Early in 1728, despite the renunciation of his project, Atterbury determined to assist the cause of his friend even further by advising him to avoid the persecution and prospect of a trial for heresy by escaping to England. There he would find a warm welcome for William Wake, the Archbishop of Canterbury, was a great admirer, and he had already been honoured by Oxford, on the recommendation of Atterbury, with a Doctorate of Divinity in August of 1727. Accompanied by one of Atterbury's friends, a man by the name of Sparrow, and disguised as a civilian, Le Courayer made his way to Calais and thence embarked for England on January 19. Before leaving, he had presented a portrait of himself to his friend, and this now hangs in the gallery of the Bodleian Library at Oxford. If Atterbury had thought for a moment that his role in the escape would go unnoticed he was sadly disillusioned. The zealous Sample had certainly made his report to the British Embassy and, according to a letter sent by Sparrow to Atterbury on Jan. 18, 1728 (Nichols, vol. V, Letter XXVIII, p. 101), the diplomats there informed the French Court. On behalf of an outraged Cardinal Fleury, the Paris Lieutenant of Police, M. Hérault, paid Atterbury a formal visit on February 14. How could someone, he declared in a polite but firm tone, who had been favoured by France's hospitality encourage a heretic to escape justice even providing transport and a guide? The Bishop protested vehemently that he had done no more than friendship and common courtesy dictated. Hérault appeared to be mollified by this explanation but, on his return to Fleury, it became generally known in Paris circles that the exiled Bishop had come into grave disfavour with the Court and that he constituted a danger to the realm. Despite a letter of defence which Atterbury addressed to the Cardinal, the latter sent a strongly worded missive to the effect that he was to be virtually ostracized especially by Jansenists and priests whose teaching was contrary to that of the Roman Church.

No trace subsists of correspondence between Le Courayer and Atterbury though it was frequent (see for example a letter from Atterbury to Mr. Williams, Nichols, vol. I, Letter LXXII, p. 170, where the former writes: 'I find neither you nor Pere Courayer understand what I writ to him'); further communication was carried out through the intermediary of the Morrices who kept both parties up-to-date about things political and ecclesiastical. Le Courayer did not apparently make many close friends amongst the British clergy probably because, as he was persona non grata in France, none of them wished to offend the powerful Cardinal Fleury or Sir Robert Walpole and his brother Horatio who were both desperately trying to maintain cordial relations with the French government. His chief friend, ally, and indeed patron was Viscount Percival, first Earl of Egmont who had met Le Courayer at Sainte-Geneviève during a visit to Paris. The Egmont diary edited by R. A. Roberts and published by HM Stationery Office in 1923, shows how close the two friends were.

The Le Courayer episode weighed heavily on Atterbury's mind, and to avoid any further unpleasantness he resolved to prove his complete detachment from the Pretender's affairs by leaving Paris and retiring to the countryside. With this end in view he succeeded in renting a small villa in the little village of Suresnes. There he rested, studied and took invigorating walks. Letters to the Morrices of late August 1728, report his catching cold in the forest of St. Germains, closely following the proceedings of the Congress of Soissons where Fleury and Zinzendorf

were the chief speakers, and engaging in a dispute with his
landlord for lack of a formal notice about leaving for more
distant parts. The Pretender was glad to be rid of a
Minister who was in such disfavour with the authorities but
unhappy at losing one of his most able advisers. Colonel
Daniel O'Brien, a young French-educated Irishman who had
acted as secretary and messenger to Versailles and who had
now been officially appointed as the new Minister in Paris,
was instructed to visit Atterbury at Suresnes to discover his
future intentions and carried personal letters from James
indicating a wish to re-engage Atterbury in his service.
However, Atterbury remained adamant; he had forsworn his
Jacobite activities and would not reconsider.

At the end of July, his spirits refreshed (O'Brien
reported to James that his temper had actually become 'doux
et humain'--R.A. Stuart, 117/57, 14 June), Atterbury made
plans to remove himself at a much greater distance from the
world of intrigue so that he could demonstrate to George
II's Ministers that, being no longer active in the Jacobite
cause, he was worthy of a pardon and a return to his native
England. This however proved to be a forlorn hope.
Montpellier was the chosen destination and, after a quick
trip to Paris to settle his affairs, Atterbury and his
household took the diligence to Lyon, sailed down the Rhône
to Pont St. Esprit and thence travelled by land to the
ancient University town which was reached in mid-October.
Although refreshed by the journey and revelling in the
warm climate which relieved if it did not dissipate his gout,
and intoxicated by the beauty of the city, he found that
prices of commodities were not as low as he had expected.
Montpellier was rapidly becoming a mecca for English
tourists and the prodigality of his compatriots had sent the
cost of living soaring. He lived as frugally as possible,
hiring just one footman, six domestics and chairs rather
than coaches. Letters arriving from James and his secretary
were left unanswered, and apart from reading in the
excellent city library, his main concerns were domestic.
Socializing did not interest him much. As he reported to
his son-in-law, he had resolved to be as little acquainted
with the French and to make as few visits to them as he
could (Letter to Mr. Morrice, Montpellier, October 15, 1728,
Nichols, vol. IV, Letter LVII, p. 170).

Word reached Atterbury that his son Osborne (born in 1705), a difficult and wayward character and a source of constant disappointment and heartache, had been shipped off to China on a merchant vessel to avoid further trouble, but worse, that his favourite daughter Mary had contracted the tuberculosis which had killed her mother and that her life was in grave danger. Atterbury had already planned to rent a house in Vitry near Paris with a delightful garden, dove-house, fish-pond, pleasant gallery and charming grotto as a meeting-place for them, but Mary's condition necessitated a warmer clime and he was advised to proceed to Montpellier. Meanwhile Atterbury had, in July 1729, gone to Vigan in the Cevennes for a month's respite from the Southern heat. The arrangements for the Morrices' travel were as follows. They would go by sea to Bordeaux, where they would meet the Bishop's servants with a carriage to take them by road to Montpellier via Toulouse. Because of raging storms however, the journey was delayed six weeks and when they reached Bordeaux Mary was desperately ill. Since time was now of the essence, a servant was dispatched to Atterbury to urge him to set out in their direction. Finally, after sailing up the Garonne in a barge (carriage travel was impossible and a hoped-for litter at Agen did not eventuate) and through the canals, the Morrices reached Toulouse where Atterbury awaited them; after a few brief hours together, Mary expired in his arms. The Bishop was inconsolable and returned to Montpellier with William in a complete daze. Abandoned in a strange country, old and infirm with no hope of a return to England, he poured out his feelings of hopelessness in a letter to Pope of 20 November 1729. (Corr. vol. III, p. 78). His reason and his religion still were there, however, to guide him through the dark vale.

In May 1730, exhausted by his grief and the enervating climate of Montpellier, Atterbury returned to Paris to live quietly in a rented apartment in the centre of the old city. The French Court, no longer as vindictive as before, was still interested in learning of Atterbury's moves however, and the British Embassy dispatched John Sample to visit him. The latter could finally report that Atterbury had really broken with Jacobitism and was anxious only to

make peace with his King and return home. This was never
to happen, and the last eighteen months of Atterbury's life
were spent amid increasing physical discomforts and moral
lassitude. Feeling death approaching, he made some attempt
through Morrice to have the British Embassy's diplomatic
seal applied to his voluminous papers, but prevarication and
disagreement failed to ensure this legacy for Britain and
Atterbury was obliged to obtain from the Garde des Sceaux,
or Minister of Justice, the promise of his seal. In the early
hours of March 4, 1732, Atterbury had a heart attack and
died suddenly. After the seizure of his papers by the
French government, his body was accompanied back to
England by William Morrice, rudely impounded by Customs
officials, but finally restored to the family for a quiet burial
beside his wife and two daughters in an unmarked grave (at
least until 1877 when Dean Stanley had his name carved
above the vault) in Westminster Abbey. Thus ended the life
of one of the most controversial figures of the late
seventeenth and early eighteenth century. His death marked
a watershed in English history. Henceforward Church power
was no longer permitted to influence popular feeling and
play such a preponderant role in politics. In addition the
challenge of the new Deist rationalism in religion and the
antagonism of intellectuals to the traditions of the past
which were increasingly viewed as uncertain guides for the
future made Atterbury's efforts irrelevant to the new order.
Despite his charismatic personality and undoubted genius for
political and ecclesiastical agitation, his flawed, excitable
character and overpowering obsessions militated against his
having any lasting influence on the Church of England.

## CORRESPONDENCE - THIERIOT

Nicolas-Claude Thieriot (Thiriot) (1696-1772), the alter ego of Voltaire to whose reputation he owes all his renown, was born in Paris in 1696. While apprenticed to a public prosecutor by the name of Alain, he made the acquaintance of François-Marie Arouet, the future Voltaire, and the two men became lifelong friends and correspondents. They went everywhere together, but while one reached the pinnacle of fame, the other, lazy by nature, lived a life of pleasure frequenting cafés and declaiming the verses of his friend. Le Sage labelled him <u>Prime-vers</u>, while in society he was known as 'la mémoire de Voltaire'. When Voltaire forgot his own improvisations, Thieriot was sure to remember them.

In 1724, the year in which Atterbury arrived in Paris, Voltaire proposed Thieriot as secretary to the Duc de Richelieu who had just been named Ambassador at Vienna. Too set in his ways to abandon his pleasure-filled life in the capital, and too disinclined to accept what he knew would be an overseas assignment, Thieriot refused on the pretext that he was preparing an edition of the works of Chaulieu. About this same time, he became acquainted with Abbé Desfontaines and introduced him to Voltaire who, never questioning his friend's judgement, seemed delighted at the thought of a useful ally. An able man of letters but of sodomitic tendencies, the Abbé turned out to be a veritable snake-in-the-grass and published libellous criticisms of his new acquaintance's work. Voltaire became an intractable and bitter enemy of Desfontaines and urged Thieriot to keep company with Atterbury rather than with the Abbé. In 1725 when Voltaire had been incarcerated in the Bastille for imprudently challenging the Chevalier de Rohan, Thieriot dined every day with him for a period of six months (Williams, vol. II, p. 411), and during his exile in England kept him constantly informed about affairs in Paris.

Thieriot appears to have acted as Voltaire's literary and financial agent, trusted by his friend, but not always scrupulous. When an edition of La Henriade was in the planning stage, he collected one hundred subscriptions, keeping the money in his own name. The profits from the publication of the Lettres philosophiques in 1733 and 1734 were collected by Thieriot while he shared with the author the revenue from the Droit du Seigneur. In 1736 he became the literary correspondent of Prince Frederick (later King Frederick II), a post which brought him twelve hundred livres salary. When Voltaire broke with Desfontaines, Thieriot's conduct was equivocal to say the least. Though he owed much to both, he took the side of neither. Voltaire was wounded to the quick, telling Thieriot that Desfontaines had taken away his friendship. This bitter blow may account in part for Voltaire's implacable hostility towards his erstwhile acquaintance but did not substantially change his feelings towards his long-time friend. He continued to lavish gifts on him to build up his meagre resources and frequently left him many of his royalties. While Thieriot acted in a financial capacity for Voltaire on many occasions, his lady live-in, Mlle Taschin, became his financial agent and saw to it that his annual income of three thousand francs was not wasted in riotous living. Although he wrote nothing himself, at his death in 1772 six years before that of his great friend, he left behind a collection of minor writings that Voltaire had entrusted to him, and this was edited and published in 1820 as Pièces Inédites de Voltaire.

A prolific correspondent, Thieriot wrote at least one hundred letters to Voltaire and many more to Frederick the Great over a period of thirty years. Only one letter to Atterbury is extant, sent in July of 1726 from Forges where he indulges in soft living and studious pursuits. Although ostensibly taking the waters for his health, he does it only 'par pure complaisance' so as not to be singled out from the others. He enquires after Le Courayer, a mutual friend, who, he hopes, is keeping the Bishop well informed about the works of the best French authors, and sends his regards to the Morrices. Finally, after wondering whether his friend is still an ardent admirer of Bossuet, he implores Atterbury to forward to his contact at Rouen, the Président de Bernières, any English work which he judged suitable to his taste. The text of this letter is as follows:

1

### Thieriot to Atterbury

A Forges, ce 27 Juillet, 1726

Milord,

  Il y a huit jours que je passe icy mon tems a mêner la vie du monde la plus delicieuse, la plus tranquile, et a laquelle il ne me manque pour etre entierement heureux que l'honneur de vous avoir ecrit, et le plaisir que j'aurai de recevoir de vos nouvelles. Je ne me ressouviendrois point de Paris sans vous, et si je n'esperois de vous y retrouver à la fin d'Octobre, je n'aurois pas plus de desir d'y retourner que j'ai eu de regret à en sortir. Ma santé est si bonne depuis mon arrivée, qu'il semble que je prens des eaux de Forges par pure complaisance et pour faire comme les autres. On prend icy deux remèdes à la fois; la dissipation dans laquelle on vit guère[a] l'esprit d'un vaporeux, et les eaux retablissent l'estomac. Je ne m'accommoderois pourtant pas[b] long-tems d'une vie si oisive, si molle, et qui n'est mise en mouvement que par la bagatelle. Un long sommeil, le jeu, la bonne chêre, les cercles de dames, et la promenade, sont encore plus sensibles et plus agréables après la lecture de Ciceron et de Virgile que sans aucun exercice d'esprit. J'avois emporté quelques livres, qui sont encore empaquetées, et que je remporterai de même. Je n'ai jamais veu le goût de la société porté à la familiarité qui regne dans les lieux où[c] l'on prend des eaux. On ne sort pas plutôt d'une partie de plaisir qu'on en recommence une autre. Voilà, Milord, un detail exact de la façon dont on se comporte a Forges. Il est aussi agréable pour un homme dans ma situation, accablé de vapeurs, qu'il est insipide pour un grand homme comme vous, melé dans les affaires d'état, et dont le loisir n'est occupé que de ce que les belles lettres ont de plus sublime et de plus delicat. Permettés moi donc, à ce propos, de vous demander, sans entrer dans aucun de vos secrets, si je puis vous feliciter sur le succes de vos affaires, en attendant l'effet des voeux de tous vos amis? Le Père Courayer[1] a-t-il soin de vous faire passer sous les yeux les ouvrages de nos meilleurs ecrivains François qui auroient pû vous echaper? Votre admiration pour M. Bossuet[2] est elle toujours constante à mesure que vous parcourés ses ouvrages?

    Si vous voyez le P. Courayer, souffrés, Milord, que je vous suplie de le faire ressouvenir de l'estime et de l'attachement que j'ai pour lui. Je vous demande en grace s'il vous venoit d'Angleterre quelque ouvrage de votre goût, et que vous jugés[d] convenable a l'usage que j'en veux faire, et que vous m'avéz paru aprouver, de vouloir bien me l'envoyer par le carosse de Rouen, à l'adresse de M. le President de Bernieres[3] à Rouen. Permettez moi d'ajouter à toutes ces prieres celle d'avoir la bonté de presenter mes respects à Monsieur et à Madame Maurice,[4] et de vouloir bien recevoir les tres humbles hommages avec lesquels je serai toute ma vie, Milord,

    Vôtre très humble et tres obeissant serviteur,

    Thiriot

Mon adresse est à Forges.

## SOURCE

Printed:     1     Nichols, vol. V, Letter XIX, pp. 72-3

                2     Besterman, vol. LXXXV, Correspondence I, Letter D299, p. 305, note

## TEXTUAL NOTES

a   This is most likely an error for 'guérit'. Nichols wrongly prints 'ou vit guère'.

b   Nichols prints 'par'.

c   Nichols has 'ou'.

d   Nichols has 'jugées'.

## COMMENTARY

1   Pierre François (Le) Courayer (1681-1776), canon regular and librarian of the abbey of St. Geneviève. See Introduction, pp. 9-11.

2   Jacques-Bénigne Bossuet (1627-1704), learned theologian, moralist and orator, Bishop of Condom, then of Meaux, and in 1670, tutor to the Dauphin. A prolific writer on history and theology he was called the last of the Fathers of the Church by La Bruyère and by Gustave Lanson, the great lyric poet of the seventeenth century. His chief works are <u>Discours sur l'histoire universelle</u> (1681), <u>Politique tirée de l'Ecriture Sainte</u> (published posthumously in 1709), <u>Histoire des variations des églises protestantes</u> (1688) which was termed by the critic Brunetière 'le plus beau livre de la langue française', <u>Instructions sur la version du Nouveau Testament</u> and <u>Défense de la tradition et des saints Pères</u> (1702), and <u>Méditations sur l'Evangile</u> (1730-1). He is the author of the famous plea: 'Hors de l'église, pas de salut, hors de l'église, pas de morale'.

Letters 7, 8, and 9 from Atterbury to Thieriot are concerned with his writings.

3   Charles-Etienne Maignart, Marquis de Bernières (1667-1717), military intendant of the army in Flanders and counsellor at the Grand Conseil. He and his charming wife were friends of Voltaire and Bolingbroke when the latter was living in exile at La Source near Orléans (See Besterman, vol. LXXXV, Correspondence I, Letter D 108).

4   William and Mary Morrice, son-in-law and daughter of Atterbury.

There are nine letters extant from Atterbury to Thieriot, mostly concerned with literary matters. None are dated. MS sources for these have eluded me.

2

Atterbury to Thieriot (1)

The Book I now restore you, gave me pleasure when I read it![1] The turn is natural and familiar, and there is an air of truth in all he says; but, I think, not the hand of a master. He tells his tale, not like a man who knows anything of the rules of writing well, but as an easy companion at a table. I say of his style, what he says of his figure, "Ma figure, qui n'étoit pas dèplaisante, quoique je ne fusse pas du premier ordre des gens bien faites...." Though not of the first (or even second) order of good writers, he is yet agreeable----I cannot possibly digest his taking notice, p. 145, of the Chevalier de Rohan's fine legs: an observation, that I should have expected rather from the pen of a fine lady, and shews that the Marquis was in his nature a little too intent on such trifles. He is sensible of it, and excuses himself in the words which follow; but that excuse serves only to shew the strength of the impression he was under in this respect, since, he had judgement enough to see the fault, and commits it notwithstanding,----
- Though I see he is manifestly piqued against Lewis XIV, and his Minister Louvois,[2] yet I am apt to believe him in all

he says of both of them. His resentment seems to carry him no farther than to give him the privilege of speaking what he knew to be true; and, as the world goes, he that allows himself to censure the great even thus far, must say a great deal of ill of them--------.

FR. ROFFEN.[3]

SOURCE

Printed: Nichols, vol. I, Letter LXXIII, pp. 171-3

COMMENTARY

1     This was Memoires & reflexions sur les principaux evenemens du regne de Louis XIV----by Charles Auguste, Marquis de La Fare (1644-1712), published in Rotterdam by Gaspar Fritsch in 1716. A friend of Turenne, La Fare was first a distinguished soldier who incurred the hatred of Louvois in an amorous rivalry, and then a poet of light epicurean verse who, with his friend the Abbé Chaulieu, plunged into a life of dissipation. He appears to have been an ardent worshipper of Bacchus as well as of Venus. Many of his verses, modelled on those of Chaulieu, remind one of Horace. Apart from the work mentioned, he produced a collection of Poésies, elegant translations from Vergil, Horace, Catullus, Tibullus and Lucretius, and an opera entitled Penthée, the music for which was partly provided by the Duc d'Orléans.

2     Michel Le Tellier, Marquis de Louvois (1641-91), the great war minister of Louis XIV, and a remarkable administrator. He completely reorganized the French army. In constant conflict with Colbert, the finance Minister, he encouraged the King's warlike inclinations and

instigated a period of religious persecution which brought misery to thousands of Protestants.

3    Atterbury frequently signed his letters in this way, Franciscus Roffensis being the Latin form for Francis of Rochester.

### 3

#### Atterbury to Thieriot (2)

Rousseau appears to me still a greater poet, the more I consider him[1]. His talents are unconfined, and enable him in every sort of writing to which he turns himself equally to excel. But the old hard words he makes use of puzzle me often (who care not to consult a Dictionary) and chiefly in his Allegories ---- Chaulieu[2], La Fare[3], and Chapelle[4], have many graces of the easy and natural style, but I do not think them so perfect in their way as Rousseau is in his; nor (to tell you the truth) do I take such pleasure in reading them. The letters particularly of Chaulieu, &c, are not masterpieces in their kind, and many of his little copies of verses have nothing extraordinary in them. The copy which touched me most is the Ode on Fontenay,

"Muses qui dans ce lieu champêtre," &c[5].

I cannot but observe, that under all Chaulieu's seeming gaiety, there is an air of melancholy which breaks out by fits, and shews he was not at ease in his own mind. He endeavours to conceal it, and acts the brave; but his readers, with a little penetration, may see through the disguise. The fears of death haunt him perpetually, and appear even in those places where he says he is not afraid of it. I should be glad to know how he died, whether with the same courage he commends in lady Mazarin.[6] I should guess not, by the observations I have made of him.

FR. ROFFEN.

SOURCE

Printed:     Nichols, vol. I, Letter LXXIV, pp. 173-4

COMMENTARY

1   Jean-Baptiste Rousseau (1671-1741), French poet, banished by the Parliament in 1707, unjustly it would appear, for his arrogance, caustic humour and proud independence. Most of his life was spent abroad, in Switzerland, Belgium and England where his collected poems, odes and satirical epigrams were published in 1723.

2   Guillaume Amfrye, Abbé de Chaulieu (1639-1720), hedonistic French poet and pupil of Chapelle whose verses he emulated. Linked with the two sons of the Duc de Vendôme (the younger Duc and the prior of the Temple), he sang mostly of his pleasures with a facile and spontaneous grace, reminiscent of Lamartine, remembering his ecclesiastical duties only occasionally. Known as L'Anacréon du Temple, the ancient lodge first of the Knights Templars and then of the Knights of St. John which became the centre of the free-thinking society of the day including the Prince de Conti and young Voltaire himself, he was included in Voltaire's Temple du Goût. The latter termed him 'le premier des poëtes négligés'. At the age of 80, he fell madly in love with Mlle de Launay, who later became Mme de Staal. A protagonist of tolerance, he professed a hesitant Deism and exalted the sensibility at the expense of the intellect. His most well-known verses are the Solitude de Fontenay, mentioned in this letter, the Ode sur l'inconstance, La Retraite, and La Goutte. An edition of his works was produced in 1774.

3   Charles Auguste, Marquis de La Fare. See Letter 2, Commentary 1, p. 21.

4   Claude-Emmanuel Luillier, dit Chapelle (1626-1686), disciple of the philosopher Gassendi, jocular Bohemian and mischievous friend of Bachaumont, Molière, La Fontaine, Boileau and Racine. A lazy, charming but superficial poet of light verse he was the author of epigrams, sonnets, stanzas, odes and madrigals written chiefly to flatter the great lords and ladies who protected him. He was called by some 'un diable d'homme' and by others 'un sympathique pochard', being singularly attracted to the worship of the wine-god. With Bachaumont, he was the author of the lively Voyage en Provence et Languedoc (1656), in verse and prose, a burlesque medley of descriptions of nature, food, and literary satire.

5   This is the first line of the fifteenth stanza of A la Solitude de Fontenay. The four lines read as follows:

> "Muses, qui dans ce lieu champêtre
> Avec soin me fîtes nourrir,
> Beaux arbres, qui m'avaient vu naître
> Bientôt vous me verrez mourir!"
>
> (Oxford Book of French Verse, Clarendon Press, 1957)

Fontenay, a small town in Normandy, was the birthplace of Chaulieu.

6   Hortense Mancini, known as the Duchesse de Mazarin. A celebrated beauty sought in marriage by Charles II and other royal personages, she left a jealous husband and emigrated to England. There she shone at the royal courts of Charles II and James II, together with her fellow exile and admirer,

Saint-Evremond, dying a courageous death in 1699.

4

<u>Atterbury to Thieriot</u>     (3)

This Book[1], I find, was written two and thirty years ago, and therefore it is no wonder that it should not be equal to the later performances of the same author. One may say of it as Tully[2] speaks of his Collection of Paradoxes; "Non tale est hoc opus ut in arce poni possit, quasi illa Minerva Phidiae; sed tamen, ut ex eadem officina exisse appareat."[3] Though it be not of the same value with his other Works, yet it is such, as that one may perceive the same Workman's hand and skill in it. He chose a little contracted subject; and not room therefore to shew his talents at full length in managing it. And yet, narrow and dry as his subject is, he has, by making several little digressions, and by taking occasion to say many things which were not necessary to his point, rendered it not only instructive but entertaining.

"In tenui labor, at tenuis non gloria, si quem
Numina laeva sinunt, auditque vocatus Apollo."[4]

Whether his fourth Gordean be a reality or a Phantom; whether he owes his very being to this gentleman, or is only rescued from oblivion, and brought again to life by him, let the Antiquaries determine: I am so easy and indolent as not to think it of much moment, which way such facts are settled; nor should I have thought what is written on this point worth reading, if this Author had not written it. In all he writes, one sees the same candour and impartiality; the same learning, good sense, and exactness. If the argument he handles be not of importance, he makes it so by his manner of handling it. So that I could wish, instead of four books, he had written forty: as old as I am, and as many other things as I have to do, I should read all of them . . . . . . .

FR. ROFFEN.

SOURCE

Printed:  Nichols, vol. I, Lettter LXXV, pp. 175-6

COMMENTARY

1   Histoire des quatre Gordiens, prouvée et
    illustrée par les médailles (1695), by Jean-
    Baptiste, Abbé Dubos (or Du Bos) (1670-1742),
    historian, critic and man of letters. An able
    diplomat he worked in the Foreign Office under
    Torcy and was despatched on several diplomatic
    missions. His most important work was
    Réflexions critiques sur la poésie et la peinture
    (1719, completed in 1733). Other works include
    Histoire de la ligue faite à Cambray . . . . . (2
    vols, 1709), Histoire des quatre Cicérons (1714),
    and Histoire critique de l'établissement de la
    monarchie française dans les Gaules (3 vols,
    1734), a well-written but controversial work,
    attacked by Montesquieu. A sceptic and
    disciple of Bayle, Dubos was a great admirer of
    poetry and the Bible. In essence the work
    mentioned here is an historical theory
    recognized as a paradox. There were only
    three Roman Emperors named Gordian, ruling
    briefly from 238-244 A.D. Nichols wrongly
    attributes the book to a M. de Boze. (vol. I, p.
    175, note)

2   Marcus Tullius Cicero (106 B.C. - 43 B.C.),
    soldier, orator and prolific Roman writer.
    Recognized by critics as the greatest enricher
    and stylist of the Latin language that Rome had
    ever produced, he is the author of four main
    bodies of work: The Orations, Rhetoric,
    Philosophy, and the vast collection of his
    Letters, which give a vivid picture of the
    turbulent Rome of the period.

3   "This work is not of such quality as to be able to be placed in the citadel as if it were the famous Athena of Phidias, yet its quality evidently indicates its source in the same workshop." Cicero, Paradoxa Stoicorum, Proem 5. Nichols prints 'ut in arte'.

4   "Slender the subject of my composition, but its fame will not be slender, if the opposing deities allow this and Apollo hearkens when called." Vergil, Georgics, IV, 6-7

5

Atterbury to Thieriot (4)

I have perused the Book about Poetry and Painting, with attention.[1] It is written in a very good goût, and has excellent things in it. I have been pleased with no Book so much that has fallen in my way since I came into France. However, I could wish those philosophical reasonings had been omitted; they belong rather to a Member of the Academy of Sciences than to one of the Forty,[2] and perhaps will neither convince nor please in such a performance. The Author seems to have gone too deep in that sort of reflections; and sometimes not to have gone deep enough in others, which relate more immediately and naturally to his subject. Forgive this freedom, but it is my real sense of the matter. Besides, there is, I think, a want of method in the whole[3]; and the 19th Section, which is so long, is to me a little obscure. The many learned citations there do not clear, but cloud the author's meaning. I am apt to imagine that, in the musical part of it, he speaks of what he does not himself thoroughly understand; for, if he does, he would probably have expressed himself so that his reader would also have understood it, which (as to me at least) is not the case. In one thing I differ from him essentially; my fixed opinion is, that the reputation of all Books which are perfectly well written comes originally from the few, and not from the many; and I think I could say a good deal in defence of that opinion ----------- I see him here, and every where, under the image of

"----Urbani parcentis viribus, atque Extenuantis eas consulto."[4]

He seldom speaks out where he is likely to offend, but contents himself oftentimes rather to insinuate, than affirm; and makes use of other men's words to express his own sense, where he is unwilling too openly to own it, or too strongly to press it. "Ab arte sua non recessit," as Tully says of Aristoxenus.[5] Even in his judgement of the Belles Lettres he plays the Politician ---- I could not but observe, how, in the last Section but one, he has furnished M. de Voltaire with the Hint of his Poem on the Ligue . . . .[6] Upon the whole, I repeat my thanks to you for the great satisfaction which the reading of these two volumes has given me . . . . .

As to Mr. Arnauld's piece, intitled, "Reflexions sur l'Eloquence,"[7] though what he says there be sensible and just; yet I do not see much of the great man in it, and had no great pleasure in perusing it.


SOURCE

    Printed:        Nichols, vol. I, Letter LXXVI, pp. 177-9

COMMENTARY

1       Reflexions critiques sur la poésie et la peinture (1719-33) by Jean-Baptiste, Abbé Dubos (see preceding letter, Commentary 1). This work, praised by Voltaire as 'le livre le plus utile qu'on ait jamais écrit sur ces matières chez aucun peuple de l'Europe', won Dubos a seat in the French Academy whose perpetual secretary he became in 1720.

The main theme of the work is that beauty is relative depending on the age, the country, manners and climate and comes from the creative personality rather than from any set of precise rules.

2   The forty members of the Académie Française.

3   In a new edition of the work, containing corrections and additions, the author changed the order and arrangement of the material.

4   The full quotation reads:
"[Et sermone opus est modo tristi saepe iocoso,/defendente vicem modo rhetoris atque poetae,/interdum] urbani, parcentis viribus atque/extenuantis eas consulto."
"[There is need for discourse now severe, often playful, now playing the role of the orator and now of the poet, sometimes] of the polished writer who purposely withholds and diminishes his strength."
Horace, Satires I, 10, 13-14

5   "He did not relinquish his skill." Cicero Tusculans, I, 10, 20

The original reads '[Hic] ab artificio suo non recessit' which has approximately the same sense.
Aristoxenus (c. 360 B.C.), philosopher, musician, and pupil of Aristotle, regarded the soul as a tuning (intentio) of the body.

6   François-Marie Arouet de Voltaire (1694-1778), the predominant writer of the eighteenth century in France whose prolific output covered many different fields of knowledge, scientific, philosophic and literary. The work mentioned was his renowned epic on Henri IV, which appeared as La Ligue ou Henri le Grand in

1723, and as La Henriade in 1728. The poem depicts the siege of Paris, the assassination of Henri III, the defeat of the Ligue at the battle of Ivry, and the entry of Henri IV into Paris. The finest parts are probably the account of the massacre of St. Bartholomew, and the vision in which St. Louis reveals to Henri IV the destinies of his country. Underlying the principal themes is the author's condemnation of civil discord and religious fanaticism.

7   A work of this title written in collaboration with Brulard de Sillery, Bishop of Soissons, and Dom François Lami was published in 1700. However, the reference here is probably to the Réflexions sur l'éloquence des prédicateurs (1695), one of the numerous works of Antoine Arnauld (1612-94), ardent theologian and controversialist, defender of Jansenism and bitter opponent of the Jesuits. Antoine was the most celebrated member of a distinguished Auvergne family which gave many sons and daughters to Port-Royal, the Cistercian convent in the Vallée de Chevreuse which, under the direction of Jean Du Vergier de Hauranne, Abbé de Saint-Cyran (1581-1643), became the austere centre and symbol of Jansenism. The work mentioned was attacked by the Doctors of the Sorbonne and defended by Blaise Pascal (1623-62), the most celebrated name associated with the convent, in his Lettres provinciales, dealing with divine grace and casting discredit on the ethical code of the Jesuits.

## 6

### Atterbury to Thieriot    (5)

I return you, Sir, the two eloges[1], which I have perused with pleasure. I borrow that word from your language, because we have none in our own that exactly expresses it. By the account I had of those pieces, I imagined them very different from what I find them. M. Fontenelle's talents, as to the knowledge of Nature, Mathematicks, and the Belles Lettres, are sufficiently understood. But I take notice particularly of the art and address with which he conducts himself in nice points, and the prudent and political views by which his pen is guided; a quality, that does not often belong to men who have spent so much of their time in studying the Arts and Sciences. He has been misinformed as to one little particular, in the short draught he has given us of Sir Isaac Newton's figure. The "oeil fort vif, & fort perçant," which he gives him, did not belong to him, at least not for twenty years past, about which time I first came acquainted with him. Indeed, in the whole air of his face and make, there was nothing of that penetrating sagacity which appears in his composures. He had something rather languid in his look and manner, which did not raise any great expectation in those who did not know him.

I see M. Fontenelle speaks warily as to the MSS. relating to Antiquity, History and Divinity, which Sir Isaac left behind him: I wish, for the honour of our country, that they may be as excellent in their kind as those he published. But I fear the case is otherwise; and that he will be found to have been a great Master only in that one way to which he was by nature inclined. It is enough for us poor limited creatures, if we remarkably excel in any one branch of knowledge. We may have a smattering of more; but it is beyond the lot of our nature, to attain any perfection in them. M. Fontenelle's praise of Sir Isaac's modesty (and of modesty in general) is to me the most pleasing part of that description he has given us of him. It is that modesty which will teach us to speak and think of the Ancients with reverence, especially if we happen not to be thoroughly acquainted with them. Sir Isaac certainly was, and his great veneration for them was one distinguishing part of his character, which I wonder (or rather do not wonder) that M. Fontenelle has omitted. His opinion of them was, that they were men of great genius and superior minds, who had carried their discoveries (particularly in Astronomy and other parts of the Mathematicks) much farther than now appears from what remains of their writings. One may apply to them, what was said by an old learned man to one of less knowledge and fewer years, who insulted him: "I have forgot more knowledge than ever you had." More of the ancients is lost than is preserved, and perhaps our new discoveries are not equal to those old losses.---But this was not what I had in my thoughts, when I sat down to write: my intention was only to express the satisfaction I had in the perusal of what I return, of which I could say more, if the end of the page did not admonish me to tell you how much I am &c.

FR. ROFFEN.

SOURCE

Printed: Nichols, vol. I, Letter LXXVII, pp. 179-82

COMMENTARY

1 These were the work of Bernard Le Bovier, sieur de Fontenelle (1657-1757), the nephew of Corneille and a prolific author whose writings anticipate the attack by the 'philosophes' upon religious dogma. A member of the Académie Française and of the Académie des Inscriptions as well as of the Royal Society of London, he was the perpetual secretary (from 1697) of the Académie des Sciences of which he wrote a history and a series of éloges the most famous of which are those of Newton, Leibnitz, Tournefort, Vauban, d'Argenson and Peter the First. Atterbury does not tell us who

was the subject of the second éloge borrowed from Thieriot. A man of wide learning and cool, unemotional intelligence, Fontenelle was instrumental in popularizing the new scientific system of inquiry and especially Newton's theories on the Continent. His more notable works, written with lucidity and charm, include Dialogues des Morts (1683), Entretiens sur la pluralité des mondes (1686), Histoire des Oracles (1687), and Digression sur les Anciens et les Modernes (1688), in which he took part in the celebrated dispute on this subject on the side of the moderns.


7

Atterbury to Thieriot (6)

The Book intitled, "Dissertation sur la Musique des Anciens,"[1] I send you back, is written in a very sensible and agreeable manner, with a fine turn of thoughts and words, as far as I am able to judge. I could wish only that the writer had been a greater master of his subject, so as to have given us distincter and fuller accounts of it, which would have left no doubts upon the minds of his readers. I am satisfied that a pen like his would have been able to express the most nice and difficult points of which he treats in a way equally instructive and pleasing, and have opened to us in dialogue the mysteries of music, as easily and familiarly as Monsieur Fontenelle has done those of Astronomy. The picture of Leontium, with which the reflections conclude, is exquisitely drawn; not only con studio, but con amore,[2] as the Italians speak of the favourite pieces of their best masters. One would think the book was written on purpose for the sake of the character at the end of it: as the most material part of a letter is sometimes carelessly thrown into a Postscript ---- I dare say Madamoiselle L'Enclos[3] was of the author's acquaintance. Hearsay could not have furnished him so lovely a description of her. There is something in the picture, that shews it was painted by the life, and not copied from another ---- One thing he says of her, p. 9. (pardon the remark) seems in some degree applicable to himself. His words are very good, and therefore I transcribe them.

"Son goût en la[a] conduisant de fleur en fleur, comme les abeilles, lui fait courir indifferemment tous les pays & tous les siecles. Mais ces sortes d'imaginations, si legères & si brillantes, dedaignent[b] pour l'ordinaire le travail d'attention. Un esprit né pour les agremens, & qui n'a jamais sacrifié qu'aux Graces, n'a garde de s'assujetir à la patience qui seroit necessaire pour comparer les beautès d'un tems avec celles d'un autre, pour étudier les rapports & les oppositions qui sont entre elles, pour les tourner de tous les sens, dont on peut les envisager; enfin, pour y rapporter la triste & penible exactitude que demande une parallele."

Let me ask you, for my own information, whether "tourner de tous les sens" be a proper phrase in that case. To me it seems to spoil the metaphor. He cites some authorities, which I am at a loss to explain; particularly p. 58. that of Varro. de Repub. Rom. l, i, c. I.[4] Sure he does not mean the antient Varro, who wrote nothing that I know of under that title. He is beholden, I find, to the long chapter of Abbé du Bos,[5] where the ancient authorities, relating to his subject, are collected; and he has made a free use of them. But my intention was, to tell you rather what pleased me in the book, than what I disliked.

SOURCE

Printed: Nichols, vol. I, Letter LXXVIII, pp. 182-5

## TEXTUAL NOTES

a   Nichols has 'le'.

b   Nichols prints 'a dedaignent', an obvious slip.

## COMMENTARY

1   This was the work, published in 1725, of François-Maurice de Castagnéry, Abbé de Châteauneuf (ca 1650-1708), diplomat and musicographer and the godfather of Voltaire. He was a member of the 'libertin' circle of the Duc de Sully, La Fare and Chaulieu. Together with the Abbé de Polignac who was Ambassador in Poland, he was present at the Congress of Ryswick in 1697. Apart from this treatise, he was the author of <u>Observations sur la musique, la flûte et la lyre des anciens</u> (1726).

2   'studiously' and 'lovingly'.

3   Ninon de Lenclos (1620-1705), famous for her wit, virile intellect and numerous <u>liaisons</u> with some of the most distinguished men of her day. Her <u>salon</u> was frequented by Boileau, La Fontaine, Racine, Molière and others, and she counted among her friends Mme de La Fayette and Mme de Maintenon. Her letters have been published and also a small volume of her sketches, <u>La Coquette vengée</u> (1659). Voltaire was introduced to her in her old age and received a small legacy to buy books. The Abbé was one of her last lovers.

4   Marcus Terentius Varro (116-27 B.C.), praetor, librarian, encyclopedic scholar and prolific author who covered nearly every domain of human knowledge. Atterbury is correct in saying that Varro was not the author of a <u>De</u>

Republica Romana. The reference may however be to his De Vita populi Romani, which is a social history of the Roman people.

5 In his Réflexions critiques sur la poésie et la peinture.

# 8

### Atterbury to Thieriot (7)

From what I have read since I came on this side of the water, I have conceived a much greater opinion of the Bishop of Meaux,[1] than I had while in England and give him readily the preference to all those writers of the Church of France which I am acquainted with. He is an universal Genius, and manages every thing he takes in hand, like a master. Good sense and sound reflections attend all he says; which is expressed in the most agreeable and beautiful manner, without any of the pomp or paint of false oratory. He has particularly the secret of knowing, not only what to say, but what not to say; the hardest task even of the most exact and excellent writers! .... But you know him, Sir, better than I; and I should be to blame therefore in attempting any part of his character, did not gratitude forbid me to return your books without giving you an account of the pleasure I had in perusing them. Even the lady's memoirs relating to our English Princess gave me a good deal; particularly that part of them, where the story of her death is told, in as natural and affecting a manner, I think, as it is possible[2]. It has such a melancholy air of truth in it, as, at the same time that it gives conviction, moves compassion; and one can no more read it, than one could have been present at the sad scene of it, without tears. I really prefer the Bishop of Meaux's funeral oration[3], to those of Flechier[4] or Bourdaloue[5]; though I think he would have wrote still better, had he imitated them less; for, by that means, he now and then heightens his expression a little too much, and becomes unnatural. I gave you one instance of that when I saw you last.

FR. ROFFEN.

SOURCE

Printed: Nichols, vol. I, Letter LXXIX, pp. 186-7

COMMENTARY

1 Jacques-Bénigne Bossuet (1627-1704). See Letter 1, Commentary 2, p. 19.

2 <u>Histoire de Madame Henriette d'Angleterre</u> (1720) by Marie-Madeleine, Comtesse de La Fayette (1634-93), renowned authoress of <u>La Princesse de Clèves</u> (1678), and a series of romances which are said to have inaugurated the French novel of character. The <u>Histoire</u>, published posthumously, is a touching account of the life of her great friend, the sister of Charles II of England and Duchesse d'Orléans who died in 1670.

3 Bossuet's funeral oration on Henrietta of England (<u>Oraison funèbre de Henriette d'Angleterre, duchesse d'Orléans</u>, 1670, and several further editions).

4 Valentin-Esprit Fléchier (1632-1710), Bishop of Nîmes, member of the Académie Française, frequenter of the society of the Hôtel de Rambouillet, the intellectual centre of the best Parisian society in the first half of the seventeenth century, and a preacher famous for the elegance of his sermons.

5 Louis Bourdaloue (1632-1704), Jesuit priest and famous preacher, the successor of Bossuet. His

sermons appealed to the reason rather than to the emotions as was the case with Bossuet.

## 9

### Atterbury to Thieriot (8)

The more I read of the Bishop of Meaux, the more I value him as a great and able writer, and particularly for that talent of taking as many advantages of an adversary and giving him as few, as any man, I believe, that ever entered the lists of controversy. There is a serious warmth in all he says, and his manner of saying it is noble and moving; and yet I question, after all, whether he sometimes is in good earnest. Pardon that freedom, Sir; I have read him with attention, and watched him narrowly. I have read all of the Bishop of Meaux's pieces that have been procured for me: and will wait for the rest, till I can have them from your hands. In the mean time, I will read worse books, that I may relish his the more when I return to them; though, to speak the truth, I know no writer in your tongue, that has less need to have his reader so prepared for him. Do you hear nothing from your friend Voltaire? Is England as well pleased with him, as it was? And is he as well pleased with England? or, does the satisfaction on one side abate, in proportion as it lessens on the other?[1] When will the second edition of his Henriade come out?[2] Will it afford us a better Monument to the memory of that Prince, and a nobler likeness, than the statue on Pontneuf? It will, if it be as well finished as it should be. For

"Non magis expressi vultus per ahenea signa,
Quam per vatis opus mores animique virorum
Clarorum apparent."[3]

But the spirit of pedantry is coming upon me; and it is time therefore that I tell you, I am &c.

FR. ROFFEN.

## SOURCE

Printed:     Nichols, vol. I, Letter LXXX, pp. 188-9

## COMMENTARY

1    Voltaire spent two years in England, from May 1726 to April 1729. Though admired by many English writers, his equivocal conduct (he was accused of being a spy) and somewhat satirical manner did not leave a favourable impression in general.

2    La Henriade, an epic poem in ten cantos, formerly published in 1723 as La Ligue, was republished in 1728 with the new title and dedicated to Queen Caroline, consort of George II.

3    "And human features are not reproduced in statues of bronze more [clearly] than the character and courage of famous men are seen in the work of the poet." Horace, Epistles, II, 1, 248-50. The original has 'nec magis' and 'aenea'.

## 10

### Atterbury to Thieriot (9)

I find the very last works of that great man, the Bishop of Meaux, are inferior to the rest; but, nevertheless, I would be master of all he certainly wrote. It is useful to observe even the defects of first-rate writers, as well as their excellences. There is an ill-natured pleasure in finding, that, as far exalted above us as they are, they sometimes sink down to our level. The Bishop of Meaux studied critical knowledge late, with respect to the interpretation of Scripture; and was never therefore so true a master of it as he was of the way of interpreting it by the stream of tradition. But, the older he grew, the more admired he was; and that led him to think himself equal to every man in every thing; and particularly to write Books in Latin, and Comments on Scripture, in both which ways I find him unequal to himself; and I dare say, that is the opinion of candid and judicious persons in your communion.

Our Friend, Father Courayer[1], has been pursued with <u>mandements</u>, <u>censures</u>, and <u>arrets</u>; nor have they, I fear, yet done with him. I am concerned for the fate of so valuable a man, and so excellent a writer, whose views, I am persuaded, were innocent and good, however, in the manner of executing them, he comes to have given so much offence. The twenty Bishops that have censured him seem to decline that part of the dispute which relates to the validity of our English ordinations. However, they have not spared the Church of England on other accounts, but have represented her in a more disadvantageous light than she deserves; purely, I suppose, for want of knowing her. They cite the Bishop of Meaux, and cite those works of his which were written expressly against us; which surely is a very odd way of representing our sentiments; just as if I should quote Monsieur Claude's words,[2] from any pieces of his written against the Church of France, to prove what she held in any doctrine of importance. I should think it became me rather to produce the Writers of that Church, and the acts and monuments of it, for my vouchers. The twenty Bishops have taken this method once or twice; and if they had taken it always, they would have been less liable to be mistaken in their representations of us.

What the Bishop of Meaux says with regard to our polity and affairs, is not always to be relied on; for he was not a master of that subject. He was a very great man; nor would he have lessened his character, not to have aimed sometimes at seeming to know what he really did not in matters that lay a little out of his compass. Excuse the freedom I take with the censurers, and the authority on which they build in relation to our matters: because I have good reason to think that they have paid a deference to it, at the expence of truth. My knowledge is very limited; and yet it would be no presumption in me to say, that I know better than the Bishop of Meaux did, what is the constitution, and what are the principles and tenets of the Church of England. But enough of these reflections, into which the mention of Father Courayer has led me.

FR. ROFFEN.

SOURCE

    Printed:        Nichols, vol. I, Letter LXXXI, pp. 189-92

COMMENTARY

1      Pierre François (Le) Courayer (1681-1776). See Introduction, pp. 9-11.

2      Jean Claude (1619-87), a learned theologian and Protestant pastor, famous for his disputes with Bossuet. So greatly was he respected, that, when he was banished from France at the Revocation of the Edict of Nantes (1685), the King himself provided him with an escort to the frontier. The last two years of his life were spent in Holland.

# VOLTAIRE

Since Atterbury was a close friend of Thieriot and Thieriot the best friend of Voltaire, it was natural that the Bishop and the 'enfant terrible' of the French Enlightenment should come into contact. In 1723 when Atterbury was in exile in Brussels, Voltaire, at the age of 29, had completed his Essai sur les guerres civiles, published the Poème de la Ligue and written his tragedy Mariamne. He had begun a liaison with Madame de Bernières, mentioned in Thieriot's letter (no. 1), had suffered an attack of smallpox and was under the care of Adrienne Lecouvreur, the celebrated actress to whom he addressed an epistle in the same year. The following year when Atterbury moved to Paris, after the opening of Mariamne in March, Voltaire's health had begun to deteriorate, and he went to take the waters of Forges with his friend the Duc de Richelieu. Three years later his friend Thieriot was also at Forges, though hardly in need of convalescence.

There is no indication that Atterbury and Voltaire met in 1724 since they moved in two very different worlds. All Atterbury's activities revolved around his duties as the Pretender's Minister; his existence in Paris was a solitary one and he was constantly spied upon. If he knew of Atterbury's arrival and exile at this time, Voltaire would certainly not have wished to get involved with such a controversial personage. He may or may not have heard of him in the early years of the century when the Bishop had attained a rank of eminence. In view of Atterbury's dislike of French rhyme, attested by the Abbé Desfontaines (see pp. 7-8), a mysterious epistle sent by Voltaire to John Dalrymple, the second Earl of Stair in 1719, may refer to the Bishop. Voltaire writes:

> "Je viens de recevoir une lettre de Londres dans la quelle on me propose de me liguer avec les Anglais pour bannir la rime de la poésie françoise. Je n'ai point voulu entamer une négotiation si difficile sans en parler à votre excellence. Je ne tiens pas
> la chose praticable à moins que vous ne vous en mêliez. Vous avez sceü si bien acorder l'esprit de ces deux peuples

> qu'il y a grand aparence que vous pouriez acorder aussi les poètes des deux nations". (Besterman, vol. LXXXV, Correspondence I, Letter D 80, p. 90, au châtau de Sully ce 20 juin 1719)

Exiled to England in May of 1726, Voltaire soon achieved notoriety, being presented to George I in January of 1727, attending Newton's funeral in Westminster Abbey in April, meeting Swift, Pope, Congreve and Gay, publishing his Essay on Civil Wars, Essay on epick poetry, both in English, and in 1728 La Henriade by subscription. In a letter to Thieriot of October 26, 1726, he eulogizes Pope as 'the best poet of England and at present, of all the world.' (Besterman, vol. LXXXV, Correspondence I, Letter D 303, p. 308). A hypothetic note in Besterman suggests that the holograph was probably given by Thieriot to Atterbury, by him to his son-in-law Morrice, who in turn gave it to Pope from whom it passed to his editor Warburton. Not so hypothetical since, in a letter to his father-in-law, Morrice writes:

> "The gentleman by whom you sent over your ring delivered that and your letter to me. One of them containing extracts of a letter of Voltaire's has (I mean the extracts) been shewn to our Twickenham friend, who could not but be pleased with them as he was at the manner of their being sent." (16 March 1727 n.s. Nichols, vol. V, Letter XXIV, p. 90 and see Rousseau, vol. I, p. 65, note 18)

In a letter to Thieriot of May 27, 1727 (from Half-Farthing, Wandsworth where he was staying in the house of a dyer), in which he writes both in French and in English, Voltaire counsels his friend to frequent Atterbury rather than Desfontaines who could be a very treacherous acquaintance. It seems clear from the wording that Voltaire had never met the Bishop:

> "I fancy the Bishop of Rochester is more amiable an acquaintance, and a less dangerous one than the priest you speak of." (Besterman, vol. LXXXV, <u>Correspondence</u> I, Letter D 315, p. 320, and see Rousseau, vol. I, p. 65)

Meanwhile, Atterbury keeps well informed of Voltaire's literary activities in England, asking his son-in-law on Feb. 14, 1728, to send him 'the piece which Voltaire has lately printed in English' so that he can pass it on to Thieriot who has learned English and wants to translate a recent English work into French (Nichols, vol. IV, Letter XL, p. 101). A month later he writes to Mary, requesting 'Voltaire's English Ode and Reflections on Epic Poetry' but not <u>La Henriade</u> which 'would be too expensive' (March 16, 1728, Nichols, vol. IV, Letter XLIV, p. 114).

Back in Paris in April of 1729, Voltaire busied himself in the composition of <u>L'Histoire de Charles XII</u>, <u>Les Lettres philosophiques</u> and <u>Brutus</u>. In the preface of the latter, a <u>Discours sur la tragédie</u> which he dedicates to Lord Bolingbroke (section entitled <u>La rime plaît aux Français, même dans les comédies</u>), Voltaire again takes up the theme of French versification:

> "Je sais combien de disputes j'ai essuyées sur notre versification en Angleterre, et quels reproches me fait souvent le savant évêque de Rochester sur cette contrainte puérile, qu'il prétend que nous nous imposons de gaieté de coeur". (Besterman, <u>Oeuvres complètes</u>, vol. II, pp. 313-14)

And he proceeds to justify rime as necessary to tragedy and an embellishment to comedy. This allusion greatly displeased Atterbury. On the back of the first letter he received from William who was then in England, he noted 'Voltaire's mention of me' and in a letter dated February 16, 1731, wrote to him:

> "Pray forget not to vindicate me, as publicly as you can, about Voltaire's mentioning me in his preface. I have done it here myself and so loudly that I believe he will scarcely venture to visit me any more." (Nichols, vol. IV, Letter XCIV, pp. 282-3)

It is unfortunate that no records are extant of any visit from Voltaire. His Discours sur la tragédie caused a great deal of interest in England and a translation was published at the head of the fourth edition of the Essay on the Civil Wars of France in 1731 entitled A Discourse on tragedy with reflections on the English and French drama. André-Michel Rousseau comments on its uniqueness:

> "L'édition est tout à fait remarquable, car ce texte est le premier exemple d'une traduction anglaise de Voltaire, si l'on néglige un chant de La Henriade publié en 1728 dans un pamphlet insignifiant dont le titre n'indique pas le contenu." (vol. I, p. 67)

In a letter dated March 2, 1731, William answered Atterbury's plea to vindicate him by assuring his father-in-law that he would seize every opportunity to justify his opinion (Nichols, vol. V, Letter LVI, p. 167). The bad weather had however prevented him from visiting Pope to do so, since, as Rousseau rightly explains, it was essentially in the eyes of Pope that Atterbury wished to prove his innocence. And as the Discours was dedicated to Bolingbroke, the real reason for this angry outburst could have been political rather than aesthetic (vol. I, p. 67). Ten years after Atterbury's death, Voltaire treats him with scant respect in a letter to Jean-François Du Resnel Du Bellay. Insisting on the Bishop's esprit de parti, he writes:

> "Le sentiment d'un jacobite emporté et peu estimé tel qu'étoit l'évêque

Atterbury ne pourra faire préférer à
tant de bons livres le livre des intérêts
de l'Angleterre très mal entendus."
(Besterman, vol. XCII, Correspondence
VIII, Letter D 2617, p. 204)

The book referred to was Les Intérêts de l'Angleterre mal entendus dans la guerre présente (Amsterdam 1704) of Jean-Baptiste, Abbé Dubos. In this work the author demonstrates that England can only lose in the war of the Spanish Succession (1701), a view belied by the victories of Marlborough at Ramillies, Oudenarde and Malplaquet. The reference above appears to be the last mention by Voltaire of the Bishop.

# CORRESPONDENCE - CAUMONT

The son of Louis-François de Seytres, Marquis de Caumont, and Catherine de Fortia-Montréal, Joseph de Seytres, Marquis de Caumont was born in Avignon in 1688. Blessed with a large fortune, he had no desire to travel and remained in Avignon until his death in 1745, collecting books, manuscripts, medals and antiques, enjoying a life of good cheer, devoting himself to the natural sciences and to literature, and forever widening the circle of his friends. His correspondents, in addition to Atterbury, included some of the leading lights of the time: Voltaire, whose works he delighted in criticizing, Président Bouhier, magistrate, naturalist and bibliophile, Président de Mazaugues of Nîmes, le Père Montfaucon, learned antiquarian, Scipion Maffei, eminent writer and ancient historian, le Père Brumoy of the Journal de Trévoux who kept him abreast of literary developments and who was a great admirer of both him and Atterbury, and Anfossi, secretary to Cardinal Fleury who passed on to him the gossip of the Court. Enrolled as an anonymous collaborator to the Journal de Trévoux, he was elected honorary correspondent of the Académie des Inscriptions et Belles-Lettres in 1736, member of the Royal Society of London in 1740 and member of the Arcadians of Rome in 1743. His writings include a memoir on the Pont Surian (Flavian bridge) which can still be seen at Saint-Chamas near Aix, a dissertation entitled Conjectures sur une gravure antique qu'on croit avoir servi d'amulette on de préservatif contre les rats, the Remarques sur le combat de Cupidon et d'un coq, gravé en creux sur une cornaline, both of which appeared anonymously in the Mercure de France, and his correspondence with Bouhier (in the Bibliothèque Nationale), with Président de Mazaugues (at Nîmes), and with other friends (in the Bibliothèque Municipale of Avignon). He died of dropsy in 1745.

The relations between Atterbury and the Marquis, though shrouded in mystery, seem to have been intimate and cordial as shown in the Latin letter appended. Since Avignon was one of the seats of the Jacobite movement in France and part of Papal territory until 1791, it is highly likely that, despite his assertion that he had finished with the Pretender's affairs, Atterbury spent some time there to acquaint himself with the latest developments. Furthermore Avignon was within easy reach of Montpellier where the Bishop lived from 1728 to 1730. In this attractive city with so many memories of former Papal splendour, he would likely have frequented the aristocratic circles of which the gregarious Marquis was a shining member. That they corresponded is proved by a remark in the Abbé de la Porte's edition of the Abbé Desfontaines's <u>Reflexions sur differens genres de science et de littérature</u> (1757). In the section on Abbé Granet's <u>Recueil de Pièces de Littérature & d'Histoire</u> (1731-2) written in conjunction with Pierre Des Molets, we read:

> "On retrouve dans les Lettres de M. Atterburi, Evêque de Rochester à M. le Marquis de Caumont, cette imagination vive & brillante, ce goût exquis de Littérature, cette politesse & cette liberté de penser qui se faisoient sentir dans ses conversations." (pp. 278-9)

Of all the letters exchanged between the two friends, the only one extant appears to be the following epistle written to the Marquis.

11

<u>Atterbury to Caumont</u>[a]

sine die

Post receptas tuas, vir ornatissime, literas non multum temporis intercessit antequam inciderim in podagram, gravem sane ac diuturnam, & periculosam adeo ut dubium aliquandiu reliquerit, an cederem morbo an ex eo aliquando evaderem. Evasi tandem sed ut miles veteranus ex dimicatione longe acerrima, qui fractis artubus, & debilitatis viribus, superest quidem, sed ita superest, ut vix se superesse gaudeat & vitam deinde ducat minime vitalem. Ea certe conditione nunc sum & tamen ut primum convalescere incipio, temperare mihi non possum, quin literis tuis urbane admodum, ut semper, scriptis aliquid saltem, quoad licet per valetudinem licet non tantum quantum vellem, quantumque oporteat respondeam.

Folardi Equitis,[1] quem uti virum egregium, & rei militaris apprime scientem suspicio, infortuniis moveor: unde ortum traxerint, quo e fonte manarint, an ea alieno errori debuerit, an suo, studiose non quaero. Peregrinus sum, istiusmodi me rebus haud ingero. Meo more vivo, & Christum colo; caeterorum Ritus ac Religiones, uti non sequor ita nec culpo. Ad ea itaque quae de hac re scribis, nihil rescribo, praeterquam id quod a Cicerone dictumst[b] quadam ad Atticum[2] Epistola ubi colloquii cuiusdam ancipitis, ac periculo proximi, quod cum Julii Caesaris asseclis habuerat, mentione facta, haec adjicit-<u>Ibi de tua aliquid sumpsi eloquentia, nam tacui</u>.[3] Liceat & in hoc, quod a te, vir prudentissime, suggeritur, argumento, mihi itidem tacere; & de iis tantum quae ad literas amoeniores spectant, sermones seramus.

Vidi paginas aliquot Horatianae illius Editionis, quam sub praelo esse tibi narratum est, aere incisas. Certe luxum illum literarium, qui ostentationi potius quam usui inservit, haudquaquam probo. Vellem idem factum esse in illo sacrarum literarum Codice Alexandrino, qui omnium quicunque nunc extant, videtur antiquissimus, cuiusque jam literae evanescere incipiunt et fugiunt oculos etiam perspicacissimos. Interest rei Christianae ut eximii illius Archetypi Exemplar simile prorsus atque omni ex parte perfectum posteris tradatur idque ut efficeret, nullum non lapidem movit Grabius[4] noster sed cum quaesisset anxie qui tanti operis expensas sustinerent, non invenit, & coactus est codicem illum non ut voluit caelatura sed Typorum communium formis instructum edere. Quod ei non licuit, licebit nunc fortasse editoribus Horatii: cuius tamen Carmina ac Sermones cum multis in locis ita vitiata sint, ut de vera eorum lectione dubitent viri doctissimi: insulsum mihi videtur tabulis aheneis tamquam ab omnibus probata mandare, de quibus lis erit apud posteros rectene an secus habeant. Quae ad margines, in fronte atque in calce

cuiusque paginae apponuntur Emblemata, nullius pene frugis
sunt; oculos lectorum prudentium laedunt potius quam
delectant; librum ipsum non ornant sed efferant: videturque
mihi Horatius eo modo editus, esse instar faeminae
pulcherrimae, quae fuco illita quamvis margaritis onusta,
vestibusque pretiosissimis, laxis & undique diffluentibus
induta, in publicum prodit, tantoque magis oculis eruditis
displicet, quanto minus ipsa conspicitur, scilicet--pars
minima est ipsa puella sui.[5] Meminisse debuerant talis
chalcographiae amatores praecepti illius Horatiani [Ambitiosa
rescindes--ornamenta][6] & id quod ille in limandis suis
scriptis semper secutus est iisdem etiam edendis praestare.

  Sed haec hactenus--restat ut Querelae illi tuae,
quam in fine literarum mihi intentas, eo modo quo illata est,
id est, amice ac libere respondeam. Fateor me quae de
Laura in Novellis Parnassianis narrantur,[7] autori eius
opusculi inserenda tradidisse, celato tamen scriptoris ipsius
nomine. Non putavi id existimationi tuae nocere posse, quod
a te profectum esse omnes latebat. Sed cum videam te
malle id a me factum non fuisse monitis tuis in posterum
obtemperabo; hac tamen lege, ut quaecunque ad te scripserim
in scriniis tuis maneant seposita, neque unquam sive sub
meo, sive nullo sub nomine publici juris fiant. Id aequum
est, quod a me postulas & tibi libenter concedo, a te etiam
me impetrare: praesertim cum tua omnia talia omnino sint
ut possint ab alio cum voluptate legi; mea autem tam levia,
tamque negligenter scripta, ut apud eum, cui destinantur,
latitare semper debeant. Vale, vir summe, & me, ubicunque
terrarum vivam; sive sanus sim sive aegrotem, sive literis te
alloquar sive sileam; habeto semper tanquam tui, ut par est,
valde observantem, tibique in omni officiorum atque obsequii
genere deditissimum

    FRANCISCUM ROFFENSEM

## SOURCE

Manuscript:   Avignon BM MS 2371, fol. 57-8

## TEXTUAL NOTES

    a   The text, deficient in places owing to creases at the end and beginning of lines, has been established with the assistance of Dr. O'Cleirigh. For the benefit of the reader, the script has been modernised: indiscriminate capitals have been removed as per Preface 4, stress accents removed, double vowels replaced (e.g. 'ii' for 'ÿ' as in 'scriniis' for 'Scrinÿs' and 'obsequii' for 'obsequÿ') and abbreviations lengthened (for example, the abbreviation for the enclitic 'que' in words such as 'atque' has not been retained).

    b   'dictum est'.

## COMMENTARY

    1   Jean-Charles, Chevalier de Folard (1669-1752), of Avignon, tactician, soldier and author of military books. His best known work is the <u>Commentaires sur Polybe</u> which appeared in an edition of Polybius (1727-30 in 6 vols.) and separately (1757 in 3 vols.).

The reference here is to his strange religious practices (he spoke in monosyllables when under the influence of convulsions at Vespers). He was one of the group of Jansenist extremists known as the convulsionaries of Saint-Médard. The imbecility and often gross indecency of the activities brought the order into grave disfavour (see Knox, pp. 378, 380 and 553).

    2   Titus Pomponius Atticus (109-32 B.C.), intimate friend of Cicero and of Augustus. His sister

Pomponia married Cicero's brother Quintus. In 88 B.C. he withdrew from the bloodshed and turbulence of Rome to Athens (whence his cognomen Atticus) where, blessed with a considerable fortune, he devoted himself to literary pursuits. Cicero constantly turned to him for sympathy and advice in difficulties both public and private. The series of letters to Atticus, begun in 68 B.C., continued until Cicero's death. His fullest biography was written by Cornelius Nepos.

3 The original reads:
'hoc loco ego sumpsi quiddam de tua eloquentia; nam tacui.'

"At that I borrowed some of your eloquence--I held my tongue." Cicero, Epist. ad Atticum, BK XIII, 42, 1, 5-6 (Bailey, vol. V, p. 260)

This is a mis-recall on the part of Atterbury. Cicero's letter actually refers to Quintus minor, the mutual nephew of Atticus and Cicero, and is concerned with a family not a political matter. However, by this transference of context, Atterbury is thinking of Cicero as being in a similar position to himself.

4 Johann Ernst Grabe (1666-1711), learned German theologian. He was tempted to convert to Catholicism as a result of serious doubts about the truth of Protestant doctrines but, unable to accept unreservedly the apostolic succession, he emigrated to England in 1695 where he became a distinguished member of the Anglican church. Nominated deacon by the Bishop of Worcester in 1700 and then chaplain at Christ Church, Oxford on Anne's succession, he was awarded the degree of Doctor of Divinity by the same institution in 1706. His academic activities included co-operation in the printing of the

Alexandrine manuscript of the Septuagint and the revision of the scholia for Gregory's Greek Testament. An account of the former, mentioned here, in which Grabe gave it preference to the Vatican manuscript, appeared in 1705 together with three specimens of his intended edition. The work was published between 1707 and 1709 in four volumes; the first and last volume were edited by Grabe himself.

5    The last six words are taken from Ovid's Remedia Amoris, 343-4, the original of which reads:

>'Auferimur culto; gemmis auroque teguntur
>Omnia; pars minima est ipsa puella sui.'

>"We are won by dress; all is concealed by
>                                  gems and gold;
>A woman is the least part of herself."

6    The original reads:

>'Vir bonus et prudens versus reprehendet
>                                  inertes,
>Culpabit duros, incomptis adlinet atrum
>Traverso calamo signum, ambitiosa recidet
>Ornamenta, parum claris lucem dare coget,
>Fiet Aristarchos - - - -'

>"A man who is good and wise will censure weak lines, will find fault with harsh lines, will mark rough lines with black from a crossed pen, will cut back ostentatious embellishments, will compel [the poet] to give light to lines insufficiently brilliant, will become an Aristarchos - - - -"
>Horace, Ars Poetica, 445-50

7    Laura de Noves (c 1308-48) of Avignon, whom most scholars agree was the Laura of Petrarch's

sonnets. Some of her portraits executed by Petrarch's friend Simon de Sienne are still to be seen in Avignon. Italian influence on French poetry, especially Petrarch's, was particularly marked in Lyons where Laura's tomb was discovered in 1535. The little work in question, in which some of Caumont's ideas supplied by Atterbury had been incorporated, and which had undoubtedly been influenced by this comparatively new trend, has not been identified.

### Atterbury to Caumont

(Translation)

n.d.

After I received your letter, most distinguished Sir, little time elapsed before I suffered a serious and prolonged attack of gout which was so dangerous that it remained doubtful for some time whether I should succumb to the disease or eventually escape from it. I did finally escape but only as an old soldier from an extremely fierce battle: he does indeed survive with broken limbs and weakened strength, but his survival is such that he is hardly glad that he survives and thereafter leads a life which is not very lively. This is assuredly my present state: and yet as soon as I begin to recover I am unable to restrain myself from giving the letter which you wrote, as always, with extreme civility at least some answer insofar as my illness allows, even though it will not be as full an answer as I could wish and as I ought to send.

I am affected by the misfortunes of the Chevalier Folard, whom I admire as an extraordinary man with an eminent knowledge of warfare. I am careful not to ask where these misfortunes began, from what source they have arisen and whether they are due to someone else's mistake or to his own. I am a stranger: I do not involve myself in matters of that sort. I live and I worship Christ in my own way. I neither practise nor criticise the rites and religions of other men. So I write you no response to what you have written of this affair except what was said by Cicero in a letter to Atticus: when he had mentioned a critical and hazardous discussion which he had had with the supporters of Julius Caesar, he added these words: 'There I took a hint from your art of eloquence, for I kept quiet'. Please allow me likewise to keep quiet on this subject which you, most circumspect sir, have proposed, and let us confine our discussion to matters pertaining to fine literature.

I have seen some pages of the edition of Horace which you have been told was at the press, engraved in bronze. Assuredly I in no way approve the lettered luxury which promotes display rather than advantage. I wish this [engraving] had been employed in the Alexandrian manuscript of the sacred writings which is evidently the oldest of all which now survive. Its letters are now beginning to fade and they elude even the most piercing eyes. It is important for Christianity that a copy of that outstanding archetype completely similar to it and perfect in every respect should be handed on to succeeding generations, and to accomplish this our Grabius moved every stone, but although he carefully sought someone to bear the expenses of so great a work, he did not find anyone, and he was compelled to publish that manuscript equipped not with engraving, as he wanted, but with the shapes of ordinary print. What was not allowed to him will now perhaps be allowed to the editors of Horace. Still, since his Odes and Satires are so corrupt in many passages that the most learned men are in doubt about the true reading, it betrays a lack of taste in my eyes to commit to plates of bronze as if everyone approved of them, readings whose rightness or wrongness coming generations will dispute. The ornamentation set in the margin at the head and foot of each page is worth very little; this offends rather than delights the eyes of wise readers. It not only fails to adorn but overloads the book itself. Edited thus Horace seems to me to be like a very beautiful woman who, once she has put on make-up, even though she is loaded with pearls and clad in very expensive, loosely-fitted and free-flowing clothes, comes out in public and the less she is herself observed, the more she displeases learned eyes--I mean, of course, that the girl herself is the least part of herself. Those who love such engraving ought to bear in mind the precept of Horace [you shall cut down pretentious embellishments] and in editing his works adhere to the practice which he ever followed in applying the file to his writings.

But enough of these matters: it remains for me to reply to the complaint which you direct at me at the end of the letter, in friendly fashion and frankly--the way in which you made the complaint. I admit that I conveyed the details which are related of Laura in the new Parnassiana to the author of that little work for inclusion, however the writer's name was kept concealed. I did not consider that your reputation could be hurt by something which no-one realised proceeded from you. But as I see that you prefer that this had not been done by me, for the future I will comply with your advice--on this stipulation however that everything which I write to you should stay hidden in your desk and should never be made public either in my name or with no name. It is fair that you grant my request since you are asking me for the same favour and I gladly grant it to you; especially since all your productions are altogether such that they can be read by other people with pleasure, while my productions are so slight, and so carelessly written that they should always lie hidden with him to whom they are addressed.

Farewell most excellent Sir, and wherever I may live on earth, whether I am healthy or ill, whether I address you by letter or keep silent, consider me always as a man who greatly esteems you--as is just--and is most devoted to you in every sort of service and obedience,

FRANCIS OF ROCHESTER

CORRESPONDENCE - ROLLIN


Charles Rollin (1661-1741), celebrated professor, author and rector of the University of Paris, was destined from birth for his father's trade of cutler, but his precocious intellect was soon apparent and led him to a distinguished career first as Professor of Rhetoric at the age of 22 and then as Professor of Eloquence at the Royal College from 1688 to 1736; elected rector in 1694, he relinquished this post for the directorship of the Collège de Beauvais in 1699, becoming a member of the Académie des Inscriptions et Belles-lettres in 1701, and 'procureur' or Attorney-General of the Nation de France in 1717. Greatly beloved by his students to whom he generously offered material as well as educational support, he was nevertheless obliged to retire in 1712 because of his Jansenist views. The rest of his life was dedicated to philanthropy and scholarship. His chief works are an intelligent Abrégé de Quintilien (1715), the Traité de la manière d'étudier et d'enseigner les belles-lettres (1726-8), an uncritical Histoire ancienne (1730-8) and an equally uncritical though charming Histoire romaine, eight volumes of which were completed before his death. An extremely modest and self-effacing man, he refused honours in later life, declaring he was merely a translator and publicizer of the most beautiful thoughts of antiquity.

Where and when Atterbury and Rollin first met is not recorded, but they most likely became acquainted during the first years of the Bishop's exile in Paris when Rollin was engaged in writing the four volumes of the Traité de la manière d'étudier et d'enseigner les belles- lettres, a copy of which he presented to Atterbury (Williams, vol. II, p. 412). They were approximately of the same age and temperament and shared the same intellectual interests. Since Rollin was not a sufficient master of English, Atterbury corresponded with him in Latin, a language in which he wrote with ease and fluency. The following letter from Atterbury appears to be the only one extant; the MS itself has not been located. Rollin's generosity, modesty, intellectual achievements and great pedagogical talents are here highly praised.

## 12

### Atterbury to Rollin

REVERENDE ATQUE ERUDITISSIME VIR

6° Kal. Jan. 1731 [Dec. 27, 1730]

Cum, monente amico quodam, qui juxta aedes tuas habitat, scirem te Parisios revertisse; statui salutatum te ire, ut primum per valetudinem liceret. Id officii, ex pedum infirmitate aliquandiu dilatum, cum tandem me impleturum sperarem, frustra feci; domi non eras. Restat, ut quod coram exequi nom potui, scriptis saltem literis praestem; tibique ob ea omnia (quibus a te auctus sum) beneficia, grates agam, quas habeo certe, & semper habiturus sum, maximas.

Revera munera illa librorum nuperis a te annis editorum egregia ac perhonorifica mihi visa sunt. Multi enim facio, & te, vir praestantissime: & tua omnia quaecunque in isto literarum genere perpolita sunt; in quo quidem te caeteris omnibus ejusmodi scriptoribus facile antecellere, atque esse eundem & dicendi & sentiendi magistrum optimum, prorsus existimo: cumque in excolendis his studiis aliquantulum ipse & operis & temporis posuerim, libere tamen profiteor me, tua cum legam ac relegam, ea edoctum esse a te, non solum quae nesciebam prorsus, sed etiam quae antea didicisse mihi visus sum. Modeste itaque nimium de opere tuo sentis, cum juventuti tantum instituendae elaboratum id esse contendis. Ea certe scribis, quae a viris istiusmodi rerum haud imperitis, cum voluptate & fructu legi possunt. Vetera quidem & satis cognita revocas in memoriam; sed ita revocas, ut illustres, ut ornes; ut aliquid vetustis adjicias quod novum sit; alienis quod omnino tuum: bonasque picturas bona in luce collocando efficis, ut etiam iis a quibus saepissime conspectae sunt, elegantiores tamen solito appareant, & placeant magis.

Certe, dum Xenophontem[1] saepius versas, ab illo, & ea quae a te plurimis in locis narrantur, & ipsum ubique narrandi modum videris traxisse, stylique Xenophontei nitorem ac venustam simplicitatem non imitare tantum, sed plane assequi: ita ut si Gallice scisset Xenophon, non aliis illum, in eo argumento quod tractas, verbis usurum, non alio prorsus more scripturum judicem.

Haec ego, haud assentandi causa (quod vitium procul a me abest) sed vere ex animi sententia dico. Cum enim pulchris a te donis ditatus sim, quibus, in eodem, aut in alio quopiam doctrinae genere referendis, imparem me sentio, volui tamen propensi erga te animi gratique testimonium proferre, & te aliquo saltem munusculo,[2] & si perquam dissimili, remunerari.

Perge, vir docte admodum & venerande, de bonis literis, quae nunc neglectae passim & spretae jacent, bene mereri: perge juventutem Gallicam (quando illi solummodo te utilem esse vis) optimis & praeceptis & exemplis informare.

Quod ut facias, annis aetatis tuae elapsis multos adjiciat Deus! iisque decurrentibus sanum te praestet atque incolumem. Hoc ex animo optat ac vovet tui observantissimus,

FRANCISCUS ROFFENSIS


P.S. Pransurum te mecum post Festa[3] dixit mihi amicus ille noster qui tibi vicinus est. Cum statueris tecum quo die adfuturus es, id illi significabis. Me certe annis malisque debilitatum, quandocunque veneris, domi invenies.


SOURCE

    Printed:    Nichols, vol. I, Letter CIV, pp. 263-5

## COMMENTARY

1. Xenophon (c430-355 B.C.), disciple of Socrates, courageous, pious, and gifted soldier, politician, sportsman and prolific author with a lucid, unaffected, and agreeable style. Exiled as a result of his alliance with Sparta, he was finally pardoned but never returned to Athens. His writings, sensitive but not profound, reveal his love for the country and rural sports and his very natural human qualities. The best known are the <u>Anabasis</u>, a prose narrative in seven books of the expedition of the younger Cyrus, son of Darius II against his brother Artaxerxes II, king of Persia and the <u>Hellenica</u> or History of Greece.

2. Atterbury had sent Rollin a copy of his <u>Sermons</u>.

3. The festivities held on occasion of the New Year.


### Atterbury to Rollin

(Translation)

Reverend and learned Sir
      6° Kal. Jan. 1731 [on the sixth day before the January Kalends, i.e. Dec. 27, 1730]

When, at the hint of a friend who is a neighbour of yours, I knew you had returned to Paris, I decided to go to greet you as soon as my health permitted. This service was postponed for some time because of the weakness of my feet, and when at length I hoped to perform it, I acted in vain; you were not at home. It remains for me to discharge by a written letter at least what I was unable to accomplish face to face and to give you my greatest thanks, which I assuredly feel and always will feel for all the good deeds (by which you have done me honour).

Truly those gifts of books which you have edited in recent years were extraordinary and a very great honour in my eyes. For I regard highly both yourself, excellent Sir, and all your polished productions in this genre of letters; in which genre indeed I quite consider that you easily outstrip all other writers of this kind and are yourself the best teacher both of speaking and thinking. And although I have myself expended some little labour and time on the pursuit of these studies, I still freely proclaim when I read and reread your writings, that I have been thoroughly taught by you not only subjects about which I knew nothing but also those which I thought I had learned earlier. Therefore you think too humbly of your work when you claim that it has been composed for the instruction only of the young. Assuredly you write what can be read with pleasure and advantage by men with experience in matters of this sort. You recall to our minds subjects which are indeed ancient and fairly well known. But you recall them in such a way that you illuminate them and embellish them, that to old matters you add something which becomes new and to others' affairs something which becomes completely your own, and by placing good pictures in a good light you make them seem finer than usual even to those who have seen them very often, and cause them to give greater pleasure.

Assuredly, while you regularly read Xenophon, you have clearly derived from him both the stories which you relate in many a passage and his very way of telling them. You not only imitate but fully equal the splendour and the lovely simplicity of Xenophon's writing so that if Xenophon had known French, I would judge that he would truly use no other words, would write in no other way on the subject with which you deal.

I say this not in flattery (that defect is far foreign to me) but in truth from the conviction of my mind. For since I have been enriched by beautiful gifts from you in exchange for which I know I am unequal to making an offering in the same or in any other form of learning, I still wished to offer evidence of my mind's grateful disposition towards you and to recompense you with at least some little gift even if very different from your own.

Proceed, very learned and worshipful Sir, to do good service for good literature which now lies everywhere neglected and despised: proceed to mould with excellent precepts and examples the youth of France (since it is your wish to be of benefit only to it).

That you may achieve this, may God add many years to those of your life which have passed, and as these years glide by, may He keep you healthy and unharmed. This is the heartfelt wish and prayer of your most devoted

### FRANCIS OF ROCHESTER

P.S. That friend of ours who is your neighbour has told me you will dine with me after the Feasts. When you decide what day you will come here, indicate it to him. Since I am weakened by years and woes, whenever you come, you will assuredly find me at home.

# BIBLIOGRAPHY

## PRIMARY SOURCES

### I MANUSCRIPT SOURCES

Bibliothèque Municipale d'Avignon (Livrée Ceccano)

    MS 2371, fol. 57-8    Letter of Atterbury to Caumont

British Library

    Additional MSS 5143    Nichol's Atterbury Collection

Cambridge University Library

    Cholmondeley (Houghton) MSS  Sir Robert Walpole

Public Record Office

    State Papers    Series 35  Domestic, George I
                        Series 36  Domestic, George II
                        Series 78  Foreign, France

Quai D'Orsay, Paris (Archives du Ministère des Affaires Etrangères)

    Correspondance Politique, Angleterre, 338-40

Royal Archives, Windsor Castle

    Stuart Papers, 5-163    James Stuart, the Old Pretender

Walgrave MSS  Earl Waldegrave, Chewton House, Chewton Magna, Somerset (1st Earl Waldegrave)

Westminster Abbey

    MSS 65007-65031 Francis Atterbury

## II ORIGINAL SOURCES IN PRINT

Atterbury, Francis
- 1  The Miscellaneous Works of Bishop Atterbury, ed. J. Nichols, London, 1789-98, 5 vols. (The 1783-1790 edition has an added title page to Vols. I-IV--The epistolary correspondence, visitation charges, speeches, and miscellanies, of the Right Reverend Francis Atterbury)

- 2  Sermons on Several Occasions ------- published from the originals by Thomas Moore, London, 1734, 2 vols.

- 3  The Stuart Papers, Vol. I: Letters of Francis Atterbury --- to the Chevalier de St. George, ed. J. H. Glover,   London, 1847

Biographia Britannica
  The Lives of the most eminent persons -------, 2nd edition, Andrew Kippis, London, 1778-93, 5 vols.   Vol. I.

Burnet, Gilbert
  A History of my own time, ed. M. J. Routh, Oxford, 1823, 6 vols.

Châteauneuf, François, abbé de
  Dialogue sur la musique des anciens, Paris, 1725

Chesterfield, Philip Dormer, 4th Earl of
  Letters, ed. B. Dobrée, London, 1932, 6 vols.

Coxe, William
  Memoirs of the Life and Administration of Sir Robert Walpole, Earl of Orford, London, 1798, 3 vols.

Daily Post, (The)

Desfontaines, Pierre-François Guyot, abbé
    Reflexions sur differens genres de science et de
    litterature, éd. l'abbé de la Porte, Paris, 1757
    (The alternate title is L'Esprit de l'abbé des
    Fontaines)

Dubos, Jean-Baptiste, abbé
    Histoire des quatre Gordiens prouvée et illustrée
    par les médailles, Paris, 1695

Hearne, Thomas
    The Remains of Thomas Hearne, ed. J. Bliss,
    London, 1966

Nichols, John
    1    Illustrations of the Literary History of the
        Eighteenth Century, London, 1817-58,
        8 vols.

------- 2    Literary Anecdotes of the Eighteenth Century,
        London, 1813, Kraus Reprint 1966, 9 vols.

Nouveau Dictionnaire Historique (1772)

Percival, Viscount (1st Earl of Egmont)
    Diary, ed. R. A. Roberts, London, HMC, 1923,
    3 vols.

Pope, Alexander
    Correspondence, ed. G. Sherburn, Oxford, 1956,
    5 vols.

Stackhouse, Thomas
    Memoirs of the Life and Conduct of Dr. Francis
    Atterbury, London, 1723, 2nd edition, 1727

Swift, Jonathan
    Correspondence, ed. H. Williams, Oxford,
    1963-6, 5 vols.

Voltaire
    1   Correspondence, ed. T. Besterman, Oxford, Voltaire Foundation, 1968-77, vols. 85-135 of the Oeuvres complètes.

------- 2   Oeuvres complètes, éd. T. Besterman, Oxford, Voltaire Foundation, 1968---

Walpole, Horace
      Correspondence, ed. W. S. Lewis et al., New Haven, 1937-83, 48 vols.

Williams, R. Folkestone
      Memoirs and Correspondence of Francis Atterbury, D.D., Bishop of Rochester, London, 1869, 2 vols.

SECONDARY SOURCES

Beeching, H.C.
      Francis Atterbury, London, 1909

Bennett, Gareth V.
      The Tory Crisis in Church and State 1688-1730. The Career of Francis Atterbury, Bishop of Rochester, Oxford, 1975

Biographie Universelle (Michaud)

Dickinson, H. T.
      Bolingbroke, London, 1970

Dictionary of National Biography

Dictionnaire de Biographie Française

Every, G.
      The High Church Party 1688-1718, London, 1956

Holmes, Geoffrey
1   British Politics in the Age of Anne, London, 1967

------- 2   The Trial of Doctor Sacheverell, London, 1973

Knox, Ronald A.
Enthusiasm, Oxford, Oxford University Press, 1950 (Reprint of 1983, Christian Classics, Maryland)

Macaulay, Thomas Babington
'Francis Atterbury' in Biographies, contributed to the Encyclopaedia Britannica, Edinburgh, 1840

Mahon, Lord
History of England from the Peace of Utrecht, London, 1836, 3 vols.

Plumb, J. H.
1   Sir Robert Walpole, London, 1956-60, 2 vols.

------- 2   The Growth of Political Stability in England 1675-1725, London, 1967

Préclin, Edmond
L'Union des églises gallicane et anglicane, Paris, 1928

Rousseau, André-Michel
L'Angleterre et Voltaire, SVEC, vols. 145-7

Sykes, Norman
William Wake, Archbishop of Canterbury, Cambridge, 1957, 2 vols.

Wilson, A. McC.
French foreign policy during the administration of Cardinal Fleury 1726-1743, Cambridge, Mass., 1936

# INDEX

Adams, Leonard   v
Alain, maître   15
Amelot de la Houssaye (Houssaie), Abraham-Nicolas   8
Anfossi, M   49
Anne, Queen of England   2, 3, 54
Argenson, René Louis, marquis d'   32
Aristarchos   55
Aristotle   29
Aristoxenus   28, 29
Arnauld, Antoine   28, 30
Artaxerxes II, King of Persia   62
Atterbury, Elizabeth   2, 14
Atterbury, Francis   ii and passim
Atterbury, Francis (Junior)   2
Atterbury, Lewis   1
Atterbury, Mary (see Morrice)
Atterbury, Osborne   13
Atticus, Titus Pomponius   51, 53-4, 57
Augustus   7, 53

Bachaumont, François de   24
Bailey, D.R. Shackleton   ii
Bayle, Pierre   26
Beeching, Canon, H.C.   ii, viii, 6, 7
Bennett, Gareth V.   ii, viii, 6
Bentley, Richard   1, 2
Bernières, Charles-Etienne Maignart, marquis
    (président) de   17, 18, 20
Bernières, marquise de   20, 43
Besterman, Theodore   ii, iii, 44
Boileau, Nicolas   7, 24, 35
Bolingbroke, Henry St. John, Viscount   3, 4, 5, 20, 45, 46
Bossuet, Jacques Bénigne, évêque de Meaux   7, 17, 18, 19,
    36-41
Bouhier, Jean, président   49
Bourdaloue, Louis   36, 37-8
Boyle, Charles   (see Orrery, 4th Earl of)
Boyle, Robert   1
Boze, m. de   26

Brumoy, Pierre, père   49
Brunetière, Ferdinand   19
Burnet, Gilbert, Bishop   1
Busby, Dr. Richard   1

Caesar, Julius   51, 57
Caroline, Queen of England   39
Catullus, Gaius Valerius   21
Caumont, Joseph de Seytres, marquis de   iv, vii, 49-58
Caumont, Louis-François de Seytres, marquis de   49
Chapelle, Claude-Emmanuel, dit   22, 23, 24
Charles II, King of England   24, 37
Châteauneuf, François-Maurice de Castagnéry,
    abbé de   33-5
Chaulieu, Guillaume Amfrye, abbé de   15, 21, 22, 23, 24, 35
Chesterfield, Philip Dormer Stanhope, 4th Earl of   8
Cicero, Marcus Tullius   17, 25, 26, 28, 51, 53-4, 57
Cicero, Quintus Tullius (brother)   54
Cicero, Quintus Tullius minor (nephew)   54
Claude, Jean   40, 41
Colbert, Jean-Baptiste   21
Congreve, William   44
Conlon, Pierre Marie   v
Conti, Louis-François de Bourbon, prince de   23
Corneille, Pierre   32
Courayer (see Le Courayer)
Cowan, E. J.   v
Coxe, William   iii
Cyrus   62

Dalrymple (see Stair)
Darius II, King of Persia   62
Dauphin, le Grand   19
Derriman, James P.   iv
Desfontaines, Pierre-François Guyot, abbé   iii, vii, 7, 15,
    16, 43, 44, 50
Des Molets (Desmolets), Pierre   9, 50
Dethan, Colette   v
Dillon, General Arthur   5
Dobrée, Bonamy   iii
Dryden, John   1
Dubos (Du Bos), Jean-Baptiste, abbé   25-6, 27-9, 34, 47

Du Resnel Du Bellay, Jean-François, abbé  46
Du Vergier (Duvergier) de Hauranne (see Saint-Cyran)
Favier, Jean  v
Fléchier, Valentin-Esprit, évêque de Nîmes  36, 37
Fleury, André-Hercule de, cardinal  10, 11-12, 49
Folard, Jean-Charles, chevalier de  51, 53, 56
Fontenelle, Bernard Le Bovier, sieur de  31-3
Forbin, Françoise de  iv
Fortia-Montréal, Catherine de  49
Frederick II (the Great), King of Prussia  16
Freind, Dr. John  2
Fritsch, Gaspar  21

Gassendi, Pierre  24
Gay, John  44
George I, King of England  3, 4, 44
George II, King of England  12, 14, 39
Glover, J. H.  viii
Grabe (Grabius), Johann Ernst  51, 54-5, 57
Granet, François, abbé  vii, 50
Gregory, Pope  ii, 55

Hardouin, Jean, père  9
Harley (see Oxford)
Hay (see Inverness)
Hearne, Thomas  iii, 6
Henri III, King of France  30
Henri IV, King of France  29, 30
Henrietta of England (see Orléans, duchesse d')
Hérault, René  10, 11
Hill, Ian  v
Horace (Quintus Flaccus Horatius)  1, 21, 51, 52, 57

Inverness, John Hay, Earl of  4, 5

James II, King of England  24

Kippis, Andrew  viii
Knox, Ronald A.  53

La Bruyère, Jean de  19
La Fare, Charles Auguste, marquis, de  20-1, 22, 24, 35

La Fayette, comtesse de   35, 37
La Fontaine, Jean de   24, 35
Lamartine, Alphonse de   23
Lami, Dom François   30
La Motte, Houdar de   7-8
Lansdowne, George Granville, 1st Lord   5
Lanson, Gustave   19
Launay (see Mme de Staal)
Laura de Noves   52, 55-6, 58
Le Courayer, Pierre François   vii, 9-11, 16, 18, 19, 40, 41
Lecouvreur, Adrienne   43
Leibnitz, Gottfried Wilhelm   32
Lenclos, Ninon de   33-4, 35
Le Quien, révérend-père Michel   9
Le Sage (Lesage), Alain-René   15
Lloyd, William, Bishop of Worcester   54
Louis IX   30
Louis XIV   20, 21, 41
Louvois, Michel Le Tellier, marquis de   20-2
Lucretius (Titus Lucretius Carus)   21
Luther, Martin   1

Macaulay, Thomas Babington   iii, viii, 1
MacKay, John   4
Maffei, François-Scipion, marquis de   49
Maintenon, Mme de   35
Mar, John Erskine, 6th Earl of   4, 5
Marlborough, John Churchill, Duke of   47
Mary, Queen of England   2
Mazarin, Hortense Mancini, duchesse de   22, 24-5
Mazaugues, président de   49
Milton, John   8
Molière (Jean-Baptiste Poquelin)   24, 35
Montaigne, Michel Eyquem de   8
Montesquieu, Charles-Louis de Secondat, baron de   26
Montfaucon, Bernard de, père   vii, 6, 49
Morrice (Morice), Mary   2, 4, 8, 11, 13, 14, 16, 18, 20, 45
Morrice (Morice), William   4, 11, 12, 13, 14, 16, 18, 20, 44, 45, 46
Murray, James   4

Nepos, Cornelius 54
Newton, Sir Isaac   vii, 31-3, 44
Nichols, John   iii, viii, 8, 19, 26, 27, 35

O'Brien, Daniel   12
O'Cleirigh, Padraig   iv, 53
Orléans, Philippe de Bourbon, duc d' (Regent of France)   3, 21
Orléans, duchesse d'   36-7
Orrery, Roger Boyle, 1st Earl of   1
Orrery, Charles Boyle, 4th Earl of   1
Osborne, Catherine   2
Ossat, Arnaud d', cardinal   8
Ovid (Publius Ovidius Naso)   55
Oxford, Robert Harley, 1st Earl of   3

Pascal, Blaise   30
Percival, Viscount, 1st Earl of Egmont   11
Peter I (the Great), Czar of Russia   32
Petrarch   55-6
Phalaris   1
Phidias   27
Polignac, Melchior, abbé (then cardinal) de   35
Polybius   53
Pomponia (sister of Atticus)   53-4
Pope, Alexander   iii, 13, 44, 46
Porte, Joseph, abbé de la (Laporte)   iii, 50
Pretender, the Old (see Stuart, James Edward)

Racine, Jean   24, 35
Ramsay, Andrew Michael, chevalier de   8
Rateau, Yvonne   v
Richelieu, Armand de Vignerot du Plessis, duc de   15, 43
Roberts, R. A.   11
Rohan, chevalier de   15, 20
Rollin, Charles   iv, vii, 59-64
Rousseau, André-Michel   v, 46
Rousseau, Jean-Baptiste   7, 22, 23
Rowell, Geoffrey   v

Sacheverell, Dr. Henry   2
Saint-Cyran, Jean-Ambroise Duvergier de Hauranne,
    abbé de   30
Saint-Evremond, Charles de   24-5
Saint Louis (see Louis IX)
Saint-Maur, Dupré de   8
Sample, John   5, 9, 10, 13
Sienne, Simon de   56
Sillery, Brulard de, évêque de Soissons   30
Smalridge, Dr. George   2
Smith, Michael   v
Socrates   62
Sparrow, Mr   10
Staal, Mme de   23
Stackhouse, Thomas   vii-viii
Stair, John Dalrymple, 2nd Earl of   43
Stanley, Arthur Penrhyn, Dean of Westminster   14
Stuart, Clementina   5
Stuart, James Edward   3, 4, 5, 11, 12, 43, 50
Sully, Maximilien de Béthune, duc de   35
Swift, Jonathan   44

Taschin, Mlle   16
Thieriot, Nicolas-Claude   vii, 9, 15-41, 43, 44, 45
Tibullus, Albius   21
Torcy, Jean-Baptiste Colbert, marquis de   26
Tournefort, Joseph Pitton de   32
Trelawny, Sir Jonathan   2
Tully (see Cicero, Marcus Tullius)
Turenne, Henri de La Tour d'Auvergne, vicomte de   21

Varro, Marcus Terentius   34, 35-6
Vauban, Sébastien Le Prestre, marquis de   32
Vendôme, Louis, duc de   23
Vendôme, Louis-Joseph, duc de (son)   23
Vendôme, Philippe, dit le Prieur de (son)   23
Vergil (Publius Vergilius Maro) (Virgil)   17, 21
Vertot, René Aubert, abbé de   vii, 6
Voltaire, François-Marie Arouet de   vii, 9, 15, 16, 20, 23,
    28, 29-30, 35, 38, 39, 43-7, 49

Wake, William, Archbishop of Canterbury   2, 10
Walker, Janice   vi
Walker, Obadiah   1
Walpole, Horatio, 1st Baron Walpole of Wolterton   5, 9, 11
Walpole, Sir Robert, 1st Earl of Orford   3, 4, 5, 11
Warburton, William   44
Wharton, Philip, 1st Duke of   8
William III, King of England   2
Williams, D.   9
Williams, R. Folkestone   iv, viii

Xenophon   61, 62, 63

Zinzendorf (Sinzendorff), Philipp Ludwig, Graf von   11-12

# STUDIES IN BRITISH HISTORY

1. Richard S. Tompson, **The Atlantic Archipelago: A Political History of the British Isles**
2. Edward C. Metzger, **Ralph, First Duke of Montagu, 1638-1709**
3. Robert Munter and Clyde L. Grose, **Englishmen Abroad: Being an Account of Their Travels in the Seventeenth Century**
4. Earl A. Reitan (ed.), **The Best of Gentleman's Magazine, 1731-1754**
5. Peter Penner, **Robert Needham Cust, 1821-1909: A Personal Biography**
6. Narasingha P. Sil, **William Lord Herbert of Pembroke (c.1507-1570): *Politique* and Patriot**
7. Juanita Kruse, **John Buchan (1875-1940) and the Idea of Empire: Popular Literature and Political Ideology**
8. Ronald K. Huch, **Henry, Lord Brougham: The Later Years, (1830-1868)**
9. C.W.S. Hartley, **A Biography of Sir Charles Hartley, Civil Engineer (1825-1915): The Father of the Danube**
10. Jeanie Watson and Philip McM. Pittman (eds.), **The Portrayal of Life Stages in English Literature, 1500-1800; Infancy, Youth, Marriage, Aging, Death, Martrydom: Essays in Honor of Warren W. Wooden**
11. Carole Levin, **Propaganda in the English Reformation: Heroic and Villainous Images of King John**
12. Harvey B. Tress, **British Strategic Bombing Through 1940: Politics, Attitudes, and the Formation of a Lasting Pattern**
13. Barbara J. Blaszak, **George Jacob Holyoake (1817-1906) and the Development of the British Cooperative Movement**
14. Karl W. Schweizer, **England, Prussia, and the Seven Years War: Studies in Alliance Policies and Diplomacy**
15. Rex A. Barrell, **Anthony Ashley Cooper, Earl of Shaftesbury (1671-1713) and 'Le Refuge Francais'-Correspondence**
16. John Butler, **Lord Herbert of Chirbury (1582-1648): An Intellectual Biography**
17. William Blake, **William Maitland of Lethington, 1528-1573: A Study of the Policy of Moderation in the Scottish Reformation**
18. William Calvin Dickinson, **Sidney Godolphin, Lord Treasurer, 1702-1710**
19. Francis Atterbury, **Francis Atterbury (1662-1732), Bishop of Rochester and His French Correspondents**, Rex A. Barrell (ed.)
20. Alan G.R. Smith (ed.), **The "Anonymous Life" of William Cecil, Lord Burghley**